Chimney sweep required for large chimney in remote country rectory: 'Nothing to it,' said Hugh, emerging with only the whites of his eyes showing in a soot-encrusted face and cycling away with the advice, 'Don't go in there until the soot settles.'

Then there was The Case of the Temperamental Cooker that filled the kitchen with choking, sulphurous, coke fumes when the wind blew from the south-west. Find a solution or else – no heat, no hot water, no way of cooking.

This lighter side of rectory life will strike many a chord. All human experience is there, some of it splendidly unique. How often does an afternoon walk with pram and child mean running the gauntlet with a herd of enormous bullocks? How rarely does a valued helper give notice – due to a meeting with a pooka?

But *Where the River Flows* isn't only about the ups and downs of daily life. It chronicles the changing year superbly and gives vivid pen-pictures of the remote area which was home to the Pettigrews. And balancing the humour there is often sadness and tragedy, affecting both family and parishioners.

Always in the background is the sound of a river – the Avonmore – which bounded the rectory on two sides, 'gentle and kind in spring and summer, when catkins and primroses grow along its banks, dark and malevolent in winter spate …'

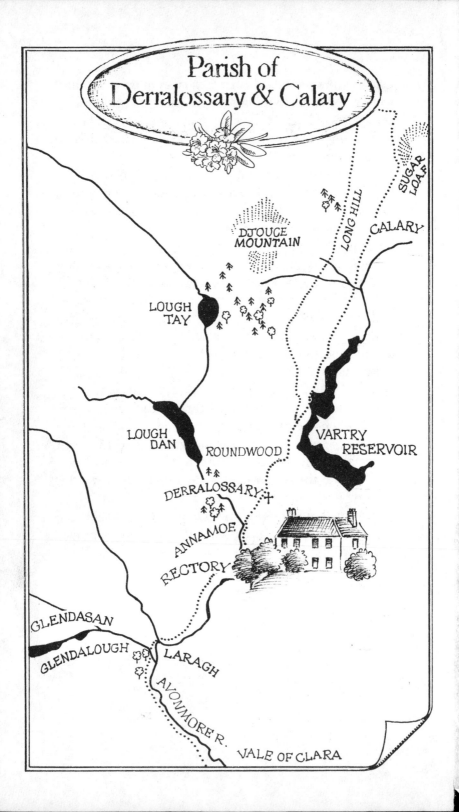

Parish of Derralossary & Calary

DJOUCE MOUNTAIN

LONG HILL

CALARY

SUGAR LOAF

LOUGH TAY

LOUGH DAN

ROUNDWOOD

VARTRY RESERVOIR

DERRALOSSARY

ANNAMOE

RECTORY

GLENDASAN

GLENDALOUGH

LARAGH

AVONMORE R.

VALE OF CLARA

LEABHARLANNA CHONTAE FHINE GALL
FINGAL COUNTY LIBRARIES

PM 8452026

Items should be returned on or before the last date shown below. Items may be renewed by personal application, by writing or by telephone. To renew give the date due and the number on the barcode label. Fines are charged on overdue items and will include postage incurred in recovery. Damage to, or loss of items will be charged to the borrower.

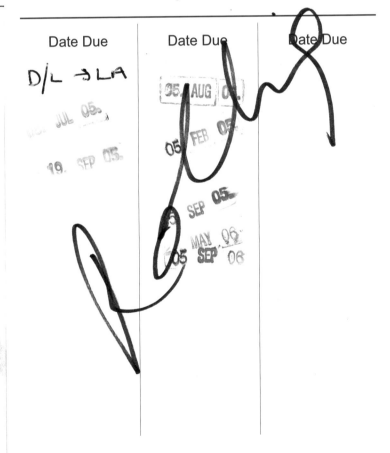

Date Due	Date Due	Date Due
D/L →LA	05. AUG 0	
JUL 05.	05 FEB 05	
19. SEP 05.	SEP 05.	
	MAY 06.	
	05 SEP 06	

To
Stanley,
our children
Judith, John and Michael,
my parents
Tom and Eva Brownell,
and all those clergy wives
who will identify with this book

First published in 1998 by
Anvil Books
45 Palmerston Road, Dublin 6

2 4 6 5 3 1

ISBN 1 901737 12 8

Typesetting by Computertype
Printed by Colour Books, Dublin
Cover painting: Annamoe Rectory by Stanley Pettigrew
Cover design: Terry Myler

Contents

Prologue

The early morning sun streamed in though the east windows of the house, casting slanting beams of golden light on the floor. Outside, a landscape of green fields and hedges stretched to the horizon. I could see the river glinting through the trees.

The sound of men's voices echoed in the empty rooms. The glebe wardens for the parishes of Derralossary, Laragh and Calary in County Wicklow were conducting a rectory inspection. As they went from room to room my husband Stanley and I followed.

The study was gloomy, with dark trees close to the window. A bookcase, its shelves painted black, covered one wall.

'Could that bookcase be painted cream?' I asked nervously.

'Why?' said the diocesan architect.

'It would brighten the room,' I whispered.

No one spoke. In the silence the diocesan architect looked back at me. 'Black,' he said, 'is more fitting.'

And closing their books, the four grey-haired men walked from the room. Their final decision was that two new floors to replace the old sagging ones and a lick of paint here and there was all that was needed. The budget wouldn't stretch any further.

As we left Annamoe rectory the sun was still shining. The air was calm with no sound of traffic or human voices, for the village was half a mile away. The heavy front door was locked with the large iron key. We all shook hands.

'Will you be lonely here?' the diocesan architect asked me in his loud, gruff voice.

'How could she be lonely?' said one of the glebe wardens.

'There's peace and quietness and good country air. What more could anyone want?'

As we drove down the avenue, the river flowed beside us, splashing and swirling over rocks and trailing branches. I looked back at the rectory. The old house seemed gentle and kind, waiting for yet another rector and his family.

1

A Leafy Island

Smoke from turf fires hung over the town of Sligo on the west coast of Ireland and the long ridge of Ben Bulben was frosted with snow. It was quiet in the rectory garden; the only sounds were of a robin singing and Craggs, the airedale, snuffling around in the grass. From the open kitchen window the smell of roasting turkey wafted in the still air. I heard the front door opening and then closing. Cecil, Rector of St John's and married to my sister Joan, was home, all Christmas Day services over at last. Someone was calling me from the house, a huge stone building with many rooms. The light from the two long windows overlooking the garden was fading as my parents, my sister Ethne and I sat down to Christmas dinner with Joan and Cecil. I remember the chill. Even though a log fire burned in the hearth that very large room with its high ceiling was impossible to heat.

A week later I went with Cecil to the parish dance. As I got ready in a cold rectory bedroom I was nervous, for this was to be my first grown-up dance. Shivering as my rose-pink *crêpe de chine* dress touched my skin, I put on my new high-heeled shoes and dabbed *Great Expectations* by Goya, the perfume much favoured by my school friends, behind my ears. Joan, five months pregnant, waved good-bye as Cecil and I walked out into the frosty night, through the door in the wall of the rectory garden and into the darkness of the graveyard, our torch briefly lighting up the ancient tombstones as we hurried past. Rounding the corner of the church we could hear the loud 'thump, thump' of the music in the parochial hall. A row of bikes leaned against the wall while the few cars were parked on the road outside.

I hung my coat in the shabby cloakroom and combed my hair in the cracked mirror. Behind me a group of girls giggled and laughed together. As I joined Cecil the band was belting out music from *South Pacific* while the couples quick-stepped by. The hall was packed because this was a special dance with all proceeds going to the Adelaide Hospital in Dublin. Balloons and Christmas decorations festooned the walls and hung from the ceiling but did nothing to soften the bright electric lights. The music stopped, the dancers parted, the girls to sit on chairs by the walls, the young men to stand together in groups. When the music began again, from somewhere in that crowded room, a tall fair-haired young man made his way to me, and that was when I met Stanley.

The dance was to end at one o'clock but by midnight Cecil wanted to go home. The church clock was striking the hour as we went back through the graveyard and the garden to the rectory.

Two days later Stanley and I had our first date, a walk with the dog. Then it was back to school in Northern Ireland for me and to the Church of Ireland Divinity School in Trinity College, Dublin, for Stanley.

That Christmas in Sligo was my introduction to rectory life. When Joan became engaged to Cecil, my friends and I agreed that to marry a clergyman would be awful! Except for one girl who had a crush on the curate. She began to write a book entitled *Life in the Rectory* and every Monday morning, during break, we were treated to the latest thrilling instalment which she had written at the week-end. As she walked home from school, her eyes scanned the roads in case the curate should cycle by on his parochial round. One day she came face to face with him and the shock was so great that all she could think of saying was, 'I liked the text of your sermon last Sunday.' Strangely, he didn't seem to remember what it had been. On hearing about Joan and Cecil she murmured, eyes raised to heaven, 'How wonderful.' But shortly afterwards her feelings began to wane and there were no more chapters of *Life in the Rectory*.

The following August I was in Sligo again for the christening of Joan and Cecil's baby son, Philip, and as his godmother I had to hold him during the service. I had never held a baby before and Philip was heavy. No sooner had the service started than he began to cry. Another baby joined in. Their shrieks rose to a crescendo while Cecil's words, as he conducted the service, were lost. My father mouthed instructions to me, my mother whispered something else, but all I did was to clutch that poor baby tighter. And the yells continued.

My embarrassment was all the greater for I knew that Stanley was somewhere in the church.

The Pettigrew family came from Sligo and Stanley's father, Keeble, a mining engineer, spent many years in mining camps in the high Andes. When the first world war broke out he and a colleague, a German engineer, made an epic journey together over the Andes, he to join the Royal Engineers in the British Army and his friend to recruit in the German Army. They never met again. During the last year of the war Keeble married Kathleen Blennerhassett from Sligo, when she was little more than a girl, and later they returned to Chile. Although she loved the warm climate, Kathleen didn't enjoy the long journeys to Valparaiso over rugged country for the birth of her three sons, Denis, Keeble and Stanley. Or the loneliness of life in an isolated mining village.

Stanley was three years of age when his father retired in 1930 and the family returned to Sligo in the west of Ireland. Some time later his father prospected for gold in Scotland and was asked by the Irish Government to do the same in County Wicklow. The original Wicklow gold-rush was in 1795 and a river that flows from Croghan mountain became known as the Gold Mines River. There in six weeks gold worth between £3,000 and £10,000 (late eighteenth-century value) was found, including a nugget of up to 22 ounces. Though gold mining in Wicklow never again achieved these peaks, it was always an on-going proposition and Stanley's father was just one in a long line of experts called in to explore for the 'mother lode'.

As Stanley grew up in Sligo the sea has always been part of his life, and that first summer I spent there was centred on Sligo Bay and Lough Gill. When we cycled down to the docks to see the boats Stanley would tell me of his great-grandfather, Captain Keeble, who owned three-masted sailing ships and sailed them himself on regular voyages between Sligo and America, and of another ancestor, Henry Bell, who invented the first steamship known as the *Comet*. Sligo has a great sea-faring tradition; another shipping family was the Pollexfens, one of whom married the poet W. B. Yeats.

Stanley's uncle had a Bermudian ketch and early in the morning we would leave Sligo to tack five miles down the channel to Rosses Point, passing the Metal Man, Coney Island and Dead Man's Point, to Sligo Bay and the open sea beyond. Nearing the Wheat'n Rock Buoy we would meet the huge Atlantic swell. With the boat rising and falling, the sound of water slapping on its bows, the rigging whining and rattling, we would sail into the wind before going about and running back to the little harbour at Raughley for our picnic lunch. In the evenings we returned home, full of fresh air, with the taste of salt on our lips and a good catch of fish. It was a new and exhilarating experience for me.

One of the friends Stanley introduced me to that summer was Bertie, a recluse who gave grinds to students at his home, Colga House, four miles from Sligo. The sun was setting as we cycled between large, stone gate pillars and down a tree-lined avenue to the old house and the air was filled with the droning of bees. As we parked our bikes by the steps to the front door, we heard voices through an open window. Bertie had visitors. Inside we sat on chairs which had seen better days. A large mahogany table in the centre of the room was piled with books, a sideboard which filled one wall was cluttered with china, candlesticks and more books, and everything was covered by a layer of dust and cobwebs. As it grew dark Bertie lit a candle and threw logs on the fire. The leaping flames cast shadows on the family portraits and the peeling wallpaper, while the flickering candle-light softly illuminated his long silver hair and white beard. Through the open window I could see the stars. I listened enthralled as Bertie talked of music, books and travel.

He had two brothers: Percy, who lived at Colga House with him and farmed the land, and Theo, who was a Consul General in Chile. By an extraordinary coincidence it was Theo who signed Stanley's birth certificate in Valparaiso.

Katie was an old family retainer who had lived at Colga House for most of her life and ruled with a rod of iron. Once Bertie took me into the orchard to 'pick an apple'. As we walked through the damp grass someone was watching us; hanging clothes on a line was an old woman, as gnarled as the apple-trees themselves. Catching sight of her, Bertie stopped short. 'No apples for us today,' he whispered, 'Katie wouldn't approve.' And taking my arm he hurried me away. 'She's really a witch,' he told me. 'On starry nights I see her taking off on her broomstick.' After that, on our visits to Colga House, when some sound outside disturbed the stillness, he would say with a chuckle, 'There she goes on her broomstick.' Often, as we cycled back to Sligo after a visit to Bertie, I was left with a feeling of another world, as if for a little while I had been touched by magic.

The flapper race-meeting, held on the broad stretch of strand at Culleenamore, was an exciting event with horses from all over County Sligo competing. As the rain poured down and money changed hands, the horses with their jockeys, bright against grey skies, galloped over the sands and splashed through pools of water. The bookies called odds, vendors sold apples, chocolate and crockery, the crowd cheered wildly and the air was electric with excitment. The races had to end before the tide came in, so all eyes watched anxiously as the sea crept nearer and nearer the course. By the last race, when the horses thundered to the finish, a film of water covered the sand. Then Stanley and I, our clothes sodden, would have a long cycle back to Sligo. Jack Yeats painted these races many times and one of his pictures entitled A *Walk Over* shows a wild western man and his horse hurtling to the finish as the crowd roared.

After that first flapper race-meeting, as Stanley and I pushed our bikes up the lane to the main road, a man standing at his cottage door called us in. Inside Matty's small dark home we removed our wet coats and drew chairs up to the open hearth. In a minute his wife had the griddle over the glowing turf and the golden cakes baking. As we drank strong hot tea and ate griddle-cakes smothered in salty butter our wet clothes steamed by the fire. When we left for home the rain had stopped but dark clouds still rolled over the Ox mountains, and Culleenamore, where the horses had galloped a short while before, was a surging sea.

Next door to Matty's cottage lived two old brothers who had spent time in America. We often saw them working their small patch, bowler-hats on their heads, pipes in their mouths. They died within a few months of each other. 'The cowboys is dead,' Matty told us when we visited him shortly afterwards. There was another sad day a few years later when we went back to Matty's cottage. It stood empty, with holes in the roof and grass growing up through the floor, for he and his wife were both dead.

Cummen, near Scarden outside Sligo town, is another magnificent strand. Fourteen stone pillars mark the way to Coney Island, two miles offshore across the vast expanse of strand, for when the tide swirls in the water is deep. On a small headland to the west stands Walker's Lodge and further west still are the ruins of Killaspugbron, an ancient Celtic church. Here we picnicked and searched for cowry shells in the sand. Flood's House on Coney Island is a landmark and can be seen clearly from the mainland.

Stanley told me the tragic story of a winter's night, many years before the pillars were built. The family who lived there left the island in their carriage to dine on the mainland, having given instructions to their maid to put a lamp in an upstairs window to guide them home. It was a stormy night when they started across the flats on the return journey and the light to guide them home was barely visible in the misty darkness. As they made their way towards it they didn't realise that the light they were following was from a cottage on the mainland at Rosses Point and not from their home at all, for the maid had forgotten to put the lamp in the window. Between nearby Oyster Island and Coney Island there is a deep gut known as *Shru na Mile*, the thousand currents, and into this horse and carriage plunged and all were drowned.

As boys, Stanley and his brother Denis had an adventure on Cummen strand. One autumn afternoon they set off over the flats to Coney Island to shoot rabbits. Half way across, the sea began to come in more quickly than they had expected and they realised they wouldn't get to the island before full tide. Leaving the pillars, they crossed the sand to the tiny grassy knoll of Inish Padraig and there, as the light faded and in the company of curlew sheltering from the rising wind, they decided to stay until the tide went out again. Suddenly, in the darkness and from the direction of Strandhill on the mainland, a strong light beamed out across the water and passed over Inish Padraig as someone who had seen the boys on the flats anxiously looked for them.

An hour or so later, from the nearest point of Coney Island, more lights shone out and a voice called, 'Take off your bloody breeches and wade.' As the tide had at last nearly receded, the two boys hurriedly left their tiny island and, splashing through the water, beat a hasty retreat along the pillars to the mainland to cycle damply home, anxious at all costs to avoid any fuss.

Lough Gill, made famous by W. B. Yeats, played a large part in the lives of the Pettigrews. Stanley's father, when young, camped with his family for whole summers on Church Island in old Crimean war tents. They regularly took part in the Lough Gill regatta and won many cups. During Stanley's growing years he and his brothers spent much time sailing, fishing and picnicking on the islands. And even though their mother didn't share their father's love of fishing, she often rowed him all the way to the head of Lough Gill, a distance of nine miles, while he trolled for salmon.

On my last day in Sligo, that first summer, Stanley and I cycled through the town, past the hospital, and turned off the main road on to a narrow track leading to the river. With Bonito, the black labrador, running ahead and the gentle swish of the tall reeds in our ears we arrived at the spot where the boat was moored. Rowing through the Narrows at Rat Island we entered Lough Gill. Sometimes the lake is rough and storms come quickly but that day the water was calm and the sun hot. With Bonito peering over the stern of the boat at the sunlit, rippling wake, we passed Thick Island and drew level with Cottage Island where Beezie Gallagher, who lived there with her herd of goats, waved to us from her tiny house. Goat Island came next and then Church Island with its horseshoe bay, ancient Celtic church and glade filled with the humming of bees. It was a long row from there to the head of the lake passing Rockwood and Slishwood under the Ballygawley mountains, setting for Yeats's *The Stolen Child*. At the leafy island of Innisfree we moored the boat and, with Bonito showing us the way, climbed through the dense foliage to the highest point.

There Stanley asked me to marry him. I was eighteen and he had just turned twenty-two.

2

Mourne Country and the Bull Wall

The Mourne mountains in County Down are a place of deep valleys, woods and gushing streams. The slopes are steep. High up, skirting the peaks, the 'brandy path ' winds its way for miles, the only sound the wind and the calling of sheep. In winter mists descend quickly and the upper slopes are covered with snow. Slieve Donard, the highest peak, rises above the town of Newcastle and it was for this parish that Stanley was ordained curate in 1950, having been advised by Archbishop George Simms to gain experience by working in the north of Ireland. He found his new life stimulating, enjoying the challenge and diversity of parish work. His rector, Canon Armstrong-Jones, was an amiable boss; the parishioners were kind.

When Stanley went north to Newcastle I went south. I had finished school and my father had retired so we returned to my parents' native Dublin. My mother's maiden name was Downey and she was born and brought up in Dublin where she lived until after her marriage to my father. He, like his younger brother Reggie, was a graduate of Trinity College, and they and George, the eldest of the family, had worked in the Civil Service in Dublin. But after the War of Independence, when twenty-six counties of Ireland became the Irish Free State and the remaining six Northern Ireland, they all went north, thinking that as Protestants they would have better prospects in the British Civil Service. Many northern Roman Catholics, for the same reason, came south.

All the Brownell brothers achieved senior Civil Service posts. George as an assistant secretary to the Ministry of Home Affairs, Reggie as permanent secretary to the Ministry of Education and my father in the Law Courts at the Ministry of Finance. When construction began on Stormont, the Northern Ireland House of Parliament, it was my father who was responsible for the planning and organising of the ceremony for the laying of the foundation stone. I can remember him leaving our home that day, resplendent in morning suit and top hat. But I think his true vocation would have been in teaching. When my sisters and I needed help with our homework he would sit beside us and go over and over something that we didn't understand. I must have tried his patience sorely for my attention constantly wandered, especially when he was explaining my sums to me, but he never lost his temper. Getting up from the table in sheer exasperation, he would light a cigarette, take a few puffs, and sit down beside me again, saying, 'Vera, you *must* pay attention.'

The fourth brother, Albert, eighteen months younger than my father, went abroad; he was an accountant in the Colonial Service in Nigeria for twenty years and when he retired he had a part-time job as accountant with the Protestant Orphan Society in Dublin. But his great passion in life was going to auctions where he would buy 'job lots'. Clocks that didn't work were his speciality and no matter how old or broken they were he could mend them. In his back garden in Killiney, near Dublin, there was a series of sheds in which he kept his bits and pieces and he could always produce anything you asked him for. On one occasion, my sister Ethne was acting in a play at the Royal Opera House in Belfast and she needed a feather from the rare African marabou stork; unbelievably he produced even that. When Stanley and I were married he helped us to furnish our flat with many of the pieces he had bought at auction, including the wash-hand stand which served Stanley as a desk for years.

On my first visit to Newcastle to see Stanley he and I climbed the Mourne mountains and walked in the beautiful

Tollymore demesne. I first heard him preach in the tiny church at Tullybranigan on the lower slopes of Donard, bird song floating in through the open door on that warm summer's day. But there was one sermon I didn't hear him preach. On a Sunday afternoon, with his robe case strapped to the carrier of his bike, I cycled with him to Castlewellan for a harvest thanksgiving service. The three-mile journey, up hill all the way, took longer than we had expected and we could hear the church bell ringing from the bottom of the final, very steep, hill. In a fever not to be late, he left me and cycled, panting, up the last quarter of a mile. When I arrived the bell had stopped, the church door was closed, the service had begun. I couldn't face going in alone so I sat on a tombstone in the graveyard until Evensong ended.

Stanley and I had been engaged for a few months when I suffered one very stressful moment. White's Milk Bar in Belfast was a meeting place for young people and on a visit to the city I went there with some of my old school friends. A girl with big hands wanted to try on my engagement ring but it would only fit on the top of her finger. Balancing it there precariously she disappeared, to my horror, into the crowd. In a panic I rushed after her for Stanley had saved for two and a half years to buy me that beautiful ring. When I caught up with her, she laughed at my agitation and returned it. Reluctantly, I thought.

After nearly three years in Newcastle it was time for Stanley to look for a second curacy. Clontarf, a large suburban parish in Dublin with a growing population and many young people, needed a curate. He was interviewed by the rector, Canon J. B. Neligan, and appointed. The following June we were married in Holy Trinity Church, Killiney. My life as a clergyman's wife had begun.

We had hoped to go to Paris for our honeymoon. Stanley and his friend Kester had spent four weeks there when students, cycling from Dieppe along the banks of the River

Seine to Paris and back. It was an epic journey. But when we worked out our budget we found Paris was quite beyond our means so we went to London and Cornwall instead.

Every evening in London we ate in Lyons Corner House in Piccadilly, where a gypsy orchestra played. Afterwards as we walked up Regent Street we would stop to look at the famous Café Royal, where Oscar Wilde once held court. On our last evening, to celebrate being married for one week, we booked a table there for dinner. As we walked through those celebrated doors the roar of London traffic faded. We were in another world of chandeliers, rich red embossed wallpaper, starched linen napkins, a very large menu, handwritten on parchment in French. The room was crowded with diners, the opulent scent of perfume and cigar smoke drifted over us. A waiter hovered nearby to take our order. But as we studied the menu, Stanley and I looked at each other, aghast, for there was nothing on it that we could afford. In the end we ordered soup but in our embarrassment, and with our poor French, we misread the menu and the soup, when it came, was iced. But the bread rolls, served with a flourish, were excellent. As we sipped our cold soup, delicious smells passed us *en route* to other tables.

The waiter was hovering again. 'May I take the rest of your order now, Madam?' He looked at us with disbelief when we declined to order anything. 'Surely a dessert?' And a trolley of spun-sugar confections dripping with liqueurs, flans and tarts overflowing with fruit, trifles, mousses and meringues was wheeled up.

'Just coffee,' I murmured faintly. The coffee was hot and strong and served with *petit four*. As we walked back to our hotel we saw the funny side of the whole situation and we laughed, tears rolling down our cheeks, all the way there.

Our first home was a flat on Clontarf Road, looking over Dublin Bay to Dun Laoghaire and Killiney, with the Sugarloaf mountain and the Wicklow hills beyond. Each morning and evening we could see the B. and I. boat, her lights shining in the dark at night, as she passed through the channel on her way to and from Liverpool. It was a good place to start our life together but as I unpacked the wedding presents and put the flat in order I began to realise what being married to a clergyman was like, for Stanley was always busy. From early morning until often late at night the demands of the parish had to be met. I joined the tennis club and the youth guild to be with him but soon discovered that as the curate's wife I was somehow slightly apart from the others. My sisters and I had been brought up to make ourselves inconspicuous, never to push ourselves forward. Suddenly I was thrust into the limelight and I hated it. To walk into a crowded church or to a function in the parochial hall was an ordeal. ' Don't leave me,' I would plead with Stanley. But he always disappeared, called away for some reason or other.

A few months before we were married something happened which should have warned me of what is expected of clergy wives. The Boys' Brigade was holding its annual display in the Metropolitan Hall in Dublin. That evening as we entered the enormous room, the captain, seeing us, hurried forward. Taking Stanley aside he spoke to him urgently before disappearing, fast.

'They want you to present the prizes,' Stanley told me. 'The person who was to have done it is ill.'

I was stunned. I had never had to do anything like that before. 'I couldn't,' I said, panic rising in me.

'I told him you'd hate it,' Stanley answered, 'but he was most insistent.'

I looked at the very high platform with its circle of chairs waiting for the VIPs. 'Would I have to go up there?' I asked.

'You'd have to *sit* up there,' Stanley replied with a smile. 'But I'll be with you.'

The display of marching and gymnastics began and Stanley and I sat aloft with the special visitors in full view of the packed hall. I barely noticed what was happening. All I could think of was the awful moment when I would have to stand up, move to the centre of the stage and present those prizes. The time arrived and the first boy strode on to the platform and saluted me smartly, military fashion. How glad I was that my long winter coat hid my trembling knees.

Afterwards I learned that no one had wanted to make the presentations and that the captain, seeing me enter, had had a brainwave. 'We'll ask the curate's wife-to-be to do it,' he said. 'She can't refuse.'

Sales are part of parish life and everyone bakes for them. The gas oven in our flat was old with no thermostat – the temperature was gauged by holding a hand inside to feel the heat. For my first parish sale I had made a Victoria sandwich. It burnt round the edges. I scraped away the black bits but it looked a mess. I would have to ice it. I had never iced a cake before but desperate situations call for desperate remedies. I read the recipe and began. After much mixing I got the consistency right. 'Add colouring if desired,' said the recipe. 'Pale pink would be nice,' I thought. I tossed in the cochineal and watched in dismay as the icing turned deep purple.

Stanley was calling me; it was time to leave for he had much to do before the sale began. Hurriedly I finished the icing and we left the flat. Walking up Vernon Avenue and along Seafield Road I glanced continually at the cake in my basket, hoping that, by some miracle, its colour would have changed.

In the parochial hall there was great activity as people prepared for the sale. I was to help on the toy stall so I slipped my cake in with the dolls and the teddies and the toy cars. Amongst the bright colours of the toys it didn't look too bad but the person blowing up balloons eyed it with distaste.

'I think that would sell better on the cake stall,' she said, so I handed my offering in there.

'How kind of you dear,' someone murmured, placing my cake, glowing with colour, amongst the feather-light sponges, the fruit-cakes and the scones. The sale began and business on the toy stall was brisk. When I next looked for my cake it was hidden behind the brown bread. Then it disappeared.

'Could anyone have bought it?' I wondered in amazement. Then I saw it had moved to the youth-club stall. I didn't follow its progress after that; it was all too embarrassing. It was a long time before I iced a cake for a sale again.

In rectories the door bell and the telephone ring constantly. It is open house twenty-four hours a day. In our Clontarf flat we had no telephone and not many parishioners called (I didn't appreciate the privacy until later).

But I did have some visitors. Stanley had been to see a retired teacher. 'She wants to meet you,' he told me. 'She's going to call tomorrow.'

The next afternoon was a blustery, damp November day and the flat was cold.

'Could you light the fire?' I called to Stanley.

'I can't,' he answered, 'I've got to teach.' And he was gone.

The match-box felt light and when I opened it there were only three matches left. I struck the first and put it to the fire; the paper caught fire briefly and went out. I tried again and the same thing happened. The hands of the clock were moving quickly to the hour when my visitor would arrive. As I struck the third and last match the door bell rang. My guest kept her coat on and refused tea; she didn't stay long.

When Stanley came home he looked at the dead fire in amusement. 'I thought you were a girl guide,' he said, 'and could light a fire with two matches.'

My second visitors were unexpected. When I answered the door two grey-haired women stood outside. 'We thought we'd drop in,' they said, looking me up and down. I offered tea. 'Just a cup,' they replied, 'no cake.' Which was just as well as I hadn't any. In the kitchen I made tea, put biscuits on a plate, poured milk into a jug and reached for the sugar-bowl. It was empty. All I had was icing sugar. Spooning it into a bowl I hid it behind the teapot and carried the tray to the sitting-room. As I poured, my guests said, 'Just one lump of sugar for each of us.' Quietly slipping a spoonful of icing sugar into each cup, I saw to my horror that it floated, powder like, on the top. In panic I gave two quick surreptitious stirs and to my intense relief it sank without a trace. But neither of my visitors had a second cup.

Another parishioner, a middle-aged woman, didn't call, but she watched our flat. As I pulled the curtains at night she would be standing on the foot-path below looking up at our lighted windows. She always hurried away when she saw me but it was slightly unnerving.

There was one person, however, who was always welcome and that was our friend Nana Grey. Generations of Clontarf curates had lodged with her, including Stanley before we were married. She was warm, kind and helpful and we valued her practical, sound advice. How glad I was to see her on the day I first attempted to launder Stanley's surplice. We had no washing machine so I washed the large linen garment in our tiny sink. I mixed the cold-water starch, added it to the final rinse, and carried the dripping surplice down to the clothes-line in our half of the garden, where it took two days to dry. We had no ironing-board so I spread a blanket on the kitchen table and covered it with a sheet. I started on the enormous stiffly starched sleeves, then progressed to the body, but as soon as I completed one section another became hopelessly crushed. It was an impossible task. An hour later I was still struggling with it.

When Nana Grey arrived, I was almost in tears. 'Send those surplices to the laundry,' she said, and after that, taking her unfailing good advice, I did.

It was Christmas and the youth guild were singing carols around the parish. In the dark we walked up Castle Avenue to Killester and along Seafield Road to the seafront. As we passed near the wooden Bull Wall bridge we could hear the sea pounding on the rocks beyond. We sang each night for a week and covered the whole parish, shuddering with cold as we stood under street lamps while the east wind whipped along the roads. The rector came too and found the note on his tuning-fork before leading us with his fine base voice. It was hard work but we made a lot of money to buy coal for the needy.

A few days later I was Christmas shopping in Dublin. On the way home a woman sat down beside me in the bus. She wanted to talk.

'Do you play whist?' she asked me.

'Sometimes,' I replied.

'I play three times a week,' she told me. 'On Wednesdays I play in that Protestant hall on Seafield Road.' Lowering her voice, she went on, 'Do you think it's a sin to play in a Protestant hall?'

'Of course not,' I replied, 'I'm a Protestant myself.'

She looked at me aghast. 'God,' she said, 'you'd never think it.'

I hadn't time to tell her that I was also the curate's wife for she left in a hurry.

Sometime during those first few months Stanley and I had our first row. Not just a tiff but a real row. To this day, I have no memory of what it was about but at the time, I know, it seemed like the end of the world. I stormed from the flat, banging the door behind me. I crossed the main road and stood in the shadows where I could see the three windows of our upstairs flat. Any minute I expected a curtain to be pulled back as Stanley looked out for me but none moved or even twitched. A fine drizzle began to fall. I recrossed the road and as I reached our front door I realised that I had left my key in the flat. I had to ring. Stanley, stony-faced, let me in. My dramatic exit ended in anti-climax.

Thursday was Stanley's day off and we looked forward to it all week. When the weather was fine we cycled along the coast road, past the Bull Wall and Dollymount strand, to the little fishing village of Howth. As we toiled up the long hill from

Sutton Cross to the summit we passed the old-world house, its garden shaped like a bellows, where my maternal grandmother, Frances Sarah (Lily) Oldfield, grew up; it was the only house on that part of Howth Head in those days. As a child I loved to hear how she rode her pony on Balscadden strand and drove the trap to Sutton Cross station each evening to collect her father, a solicitor, returning home from the city.

One story she told me was about a visiting aunt who brought her and her sisters pinafores to wear over their dresses to keep them clean. The little girls hated these garments and hid them amongst the rocks on the strand below their house. Consternation, but also delight, followed when the tide came in and the pinafores disappeared out to sea. Needless to say they were severely reprimanded.

My grandmother was in worse trouble a few years later. As a young woman she became bored with life on Howth Head and found herself a job in an exclusive milliners in Grafton Street in Dublin (the premises later became the well-known Slynes dress shop – long since vanished). Her family disapproved greatly of what she had done and her brothers refused to speak to her for quite some time. But when she married Robert Downey, who was manager of Williams and Woods, another firm which has disappeared, she was forgiven.

One hot July day Stanley and I left our bikes at Red Rock and walked through the meadows to a tiny cove for a swim. The heat was intense and I remember how the sea shimmered and danced with light. As we cycled home I began to feel unwell.

For some time I had noticed a strange phenomenon amongst the women, usually middle-aged, of the parish; every time they met me their eyes would invariably stray to the region of my stomach. Soon there would be something for them to see for I was going to have a baby. That summer the sun shone day after day and I felt more and more ill; all I wanted to do was to lie down in a cool room and sleep. But when it turned to autumn and the heat grew less intense, I began to recover. The baby was due in mid March but ten days early she was on the move. As we left the flat that evening a car full of young people, going to the tennis-club dance, passed and word spread quickly round the parish that the curate's baby was on its way.

The birth was long and hard – I had no idea there would, or could, be such pain – and it was late the following day before our daughter was born. Little did I realise, when I returned home as a mother, that my life would have changed for ever. Judith was a beautiful baby but oh! how she cried. Night after night we walked the bedroom floor with her and as dawn came we would hear the 'clip, clop' of the milkman's horse and the clink of bottles on our doorstep. How I envied that milkman as he trotted away with his horse and cart. The days passed in a blur of baby feeds, washing nappies and tiny garments. Often I would stand at the window, with Judith in my arms, looking out at the traffic, feeling isolated and detached from everyday life.

My friend Myra, a medical student at Trinity College, came to see me and for a short time I slipped back into the past. But as she left for some exciting social event, driving her own car, the baby began to cry again. Motherhood, it seemed, had taken over my life. But those difficult early days passed and as I adapted to my new role, the joy our baby daughter gave us grew. For her first Christmas we put a little tree in our sitting-room hung with tinsel and decorations and a golden star at the top. Every morning Stanley carried her in to see it. ' Twinkle, twinkle, little star,' he sang and she would stretch out her tiny hands to the bright baubles.

Clontarf Musical Society was staging Gilbert and Sullivan's *Mikado*, and for the third year running Stanley was painting the scenery. Every afternoon I pushed Judith in her pram to the parochial hall to watch him. He painted the two sets, 24 feet long by 12 feet high, and the four side flats with a very large brush and tins of emulsion paint, leaping on and off the stage to survey his work from a distance. Judith was starting to walk and she trotted around giving little shouts, for there was a lovely echo in the large empty hall. On opening night Stanley and I sat in the audience in nervous anticipation as the curtain rose on the first act. It was an exciting moment when his beautiful scenery of Japanese bridges, rivers, mountains and hanging flowers was revealed in all its oriental glory.

Not long ago Clontarf Musical Society celebrated its fortieth anniversary with a performance of *The Mikado* and Stanley's scenery, which had been used many times in the intervening years, was brought out once again – the best compliment he could have been paid.

3
A Farewell

We were very happy in Clontarf but Stanley had been curate there for over four years. Soon he was due to have a parish of his own. One Sunday Canon Neligan told him, 'I think we had nominators in church today.' The following week he received a letter from the United Parishes of Derralossary and Calary in County Wicklow inviting him to visit Mr J.B. Wynne of Glendalough. My presence was also requested.

On a perfect June day we took the St Kevin's bus to Glendalough. At Kilmacanogue it left the main road and crawled up the Long Hill. Below us the countryside stretched in a patchwork of fields with cottages dotting the landscape, the spire of Enniskerry Church and the roof of Powerscourt House in the distance. As the bus reached the top of the Long Hill, the Sugarloaf rose above us, its conical top lit by the morning sun. Sheep grazed the slopes while a farmer, dog at heel, walked the grass verge. Then the countryside changed, with Calary bog stretching as far as the eye could see. The bus stopped often as women with baskets and old men in heavy boots got on and off. We saw few houses; they were mostly hidden up rough tracks. We passed Calary Church among pine-trees and came to the village of Roundwood, sleepy in the morning sunshine. The few shops were still shut and not many people were about. The bus stopped, the driver left the wheel, and leaning on the bonnet he chatted to someone. No one, it seemed, was in a hurry.

At last we were on the move again. We saw the tower of the ancient church of Derralossary and the turf-brown Avonmore River as it flowed on its way from the Wicklow mountains. Round the corner past Brady's Glen, with

Ballenacorbeg hill rising steeply to the left, and we were approaching the tiny village of Annamoe. Over the humpback bridge with the river tumbling beneath, past the post-office, the one shop, a few whitewashed cottages with flower gardens, up the hill and we were on the straight to Laragh. The countryside had changed again, for here the fields rolled to a backdrop of tree-covered hills and we caught glimpses of large, old houses. Through Laragh we trundled, past St John's Church and down into Glendalough.

We left the bus at the Royal Hotel. A car was parked close by and an elderly man with thinning hair and steel-rimmed glasses stepped out and introduced himself. It was Mr Wynne. We drove the short distance to a lovely, old-world house where his wife, waiting on the doorstep, welcomed us. During lunch in the white-walled dining-room, with Avoca handwoven tweed curtains at the windows, she did her best to put us at our ease. We drank coffee in the drawing-room, overlooking the Lower Lake, and afterwards Mr Wynne and Stanley left us. I could see them walking up and down on the lawn, deep in conversation, and I knew that the real interview had begun. Mrs Wynne talked to me in the kindest way but I knew that I too was being 'vetted'.

Both interviews must have been satisfactory because not long after our visit Stanley received a letter offering him the incumbency of the United Parishes of Derralossary and Calary with an annual stipend of £550. He was pleased to accept, for rectorships for young men in the United Dioceses of Dublin, Glendalough and Kildare were few and in those days if you moved out of that jurisdiction it was difficult to get back.

And so the job of dismantling our home began. As we packed boxes and cases and threw out rubbish, I was worried. How would our two cats and hedgehog survive the move?

One evening shortly after we were married, Stanley, cycling home along Vernon Avenue, saw a hedgehog in the middle of the road. He picked the little creature up, tied him in his handkerchief and brought him home. We offered him bread and milk and after a while he unfurled and drank hungrily. He was an enchanting little animal with a long, damp nose and bright beady eyes. That night we left him in the kitchen – which was something of a mistake. Hedgehogs are nocturnal, so he spent the whole night on the move. In the morning the kitchen was a shambles; brushes knocked over, newspapers torn to shreds, and a trail of bread and milk across the floor. He had walked through the coal-bucket and his tiny black paw-marks were everywhere. We carried him down to our walled back garden and hoped that he would stay with us. Every evening at dusk we fed him and as we put out his food we could hear him crunching snails in our vegetable patch. 'Hedgie, Hedgie,' we would call and he would appear beside us in seconds for he could move fast. If we were late with his food he called *us* and if the back door was left open he came in. The Kellys lived in the ground-floor flat and they once found him in their bed! One evening we arrived home very late and Mrs Kelly told us, 'That creature has been roaring like a lion for hours!'

In autumn, Hedgie grew lethargic. Often he didn't come for his supper and we would find him curled up under the brussels sprouts, asleep. Stanley built a cave for him, lined it with leaves, and there Hedgie hibernated every winter. During the cold dark months, wondering if he was alive, we would kneel down, put an ear to the entrance and listen. It was exciting to hear the sound of a snuffling snore. On the first warm spring day he would appear and eat voraciously. The week before we moved, he disappeared; someone had left the gate at the bottom of the garden open. We searched for him hard and long but we never found him. We were saddened to lose him but felt privileged that he had shared our life for three years.

Puss, a big, black, cat with a white waistcoat, belonged to the Kellys. When Mrs Kelly died and her husband moved away we inherited her. 'Puss is getting fat,' I told Stanley. Each day she grew bigger and we realised that she was pregnant. So was I and we continued our pregnancies together. But she got there first. One morning, without any fuss, she presented us with six beautiful kittens. That was the first of her many pregnancies while she lived with us. She was a wonderful mother but we had a problem. We asked the vet's advice. 'She's too old to spay,' he said. That year she had *three* litters. Each brought moments of heart-break. The kittens we couldn't find homes for had to be humanely put to sleep. The alternative was to put Puss to sleep and that I couldn't do but I felt anger against those owners who didn't bother to have their tom-cats neutered.

One warm summer's day Puss was sitting outside in the garden when, through the open kitchen window, I heard pitiful miaowing. A kitten was caught in the string-frame of the runner beans while Puss, seemingly quite unconcerned, sat near by washing herself. I hurried to the rescue. As I bent over the strings to release the dangling kitten, something hit me in the small of the back. Before I could even look round another blow fell. Shocked, I straightened up as Puss sprang again. I lifted my arm to defend myself and her claws tore my flesh. I was afraid now, for each time I flung her away she bounced straight back. 'Help!' I called but there was no one to hear. I ran. Upstairs in our kitchen I bathed my bleeding arm. Then I thought of Judith, asleep in her pram at the bottom of the garden. Would Puss attack her too? Fearful, I rushed outside again. Puss was sitting in the sunlight washing, her kitten beside her. When she saw me she rubbed against my legs, purring. Over the years I have been bitten by dogs, a rabbit, a hamster and a baby rat. I have been stood on by horses and donkeys, pecked by birds and threatened by a stallion. I never expected to be savaged by my own cat. But I understood and forgave her and we remained good friends.

And so we prepared to leave our first home, with its views across the bay to Dun Laoghaire and Killiney, the sound of ships hooting in the channel, street lights shining on the pavement, cars and buses passing, shops and people.

I felt sadness that our time in Clontarf had ended.

4

The Ford of the Cows

The removal van was late on the bright August day that we left Clontarf. Stanley was still waiting for it when Judith, the two cats and I drove in my parents' car to their house in Dalkey. A few hours later we were on the road again, this time to Annamoe. As we reached Calary bog, Puss, in her cardboard box, became restless, her cries growing louder and louder. Suddenly, a mini explosion erupted and the car was filled with a strong pungent smell. We opened the windows wide and Puss, smelling the air and freedom, gave a herculean leap out of her box and through an open window, to disappear into the bog. We could see her peeping over clumps of heather at us, but when we got close away she would go again. She was very upset and so were we. At last, after many attempts, my father caught her but he had the scratches on his hands for days. As we drove off again the removal van passed us and from his seat beside the driver Stanley waved.

When we neared Annamoe the bright day had gone and the sky was overcast. We crossed the humpback bridge and turned down by the river. Beyond the rectory gate a group of bullocks watched as we opened and closed it behind us. We could hear the river close by as we drove up the long avenue to the second gate. Open and close that one too. The removal van was parked outside the front door while inside the house echoed with sound as we made our way through the large empty hall to the kitchen. Someone had lit the Rayburn and the room, with its dingy fawn-coloured linoleum, was warm. Judith's pram and high chair stood in a corner and our kitchen table and four chairs fitted along a wall. The wooden cupboard, bought at an auction and given to us by my Uncle Albert, completed the furnishing. There were no other cupboards or work-tops of any kind, just an open shelf for saucepans under the sink. It was a kitchen without any mod cons at all.

Stanley carried Puss and her son Teddy down the creaking stairs to the basement where they would be safe for the night. While my mother and I made up beds, Judith sat on my father's knee before the Rayburn. 'Go home now,' she said from time to time. We worked all evening and when the light faded and it grew dark, exhausted, we went to bed. As I tucked Judith into her cot she murmured sleepily, 'Ju-Ju's own bed.' Now *her* world was all right. I fell asleep to the sound of rain beating on the curtainless windows; outside not a single light showed in the darkness.

In the morning the sun was shining and our spirits lifted but as we unpacked we couldn't believe how little furniture we had, especially as the house revealed an enormous amount of space. On one side of the hall was the drawing-room which became our main living room. Our Clontarf sitting-room had been cosy, with a red carpet on the floor, but in Annamoe that same carpet was a tiny red dot surrounded by acres of bare floor boards. Beyond it was the dining-room – we had no furniture for that at all. And not much for the dark study with the black bookcase which, to our amazement, had been painted cream. Down two steps from the hall was the kitchen. A rickety staircase led to the basement which covered the whole area of the house.

On the top floor were four bedrooms, two of them very large. In Clontarf our furniture had filled our bedroom; our Annamoe bedroom looked stark and empty. There was one bathroom, half way up the stairs, off a bright landing, with a window looking over the fields. No frosted glass was needed there for only the birds could see in. The black and white linoleum, the plastic curtains and the other bathroom fittings came, we thought, with the house, We were wrong. Some weeks later we received a letter from the previous rector, informing us that all the bathroom fittings and the dingy floor-covering in the kitchen had been bought by him. He enclosed a large bill for us. Nowadays, parishes provide their rectories with fitted kitchens, floor-covering and cookers, carpets for the hall, landing and stairs, while the principal downstairs rooms are both carpeted and curtained. In those far off days, not even the basic necessities were provided in Annamoe rectory.

Mid morning, on that first day, we heard the sound of a tractor coming up the avenue. It parked outside the gate and the driver walked to the front door, her arms full of vegetables. It was Phoebe who lived at nearby Avonmore House and farmed the large estate. Many months later we learned that it was *she* who had insisted on the black bookcase being painted cream; she had heard of my request and was angered by the refusal. Our next visitor was Mr Wynne and he was in a hurry. 'Settling in all right?' he asked. 'Rayburn working well?' And he was gone. In the afternoon Colonel Angus Glendinning and his wife Sybil walked from their home across the river to see us. We didn't know then how important they would become in our lives.

Later that day my father explored the large garden and came back with a grave face. 'There's something you must see,' he told us. At the front of the house the lawn sloped steeply down to the basement but at the back there was a sheer ten-foot drop to large stone slabs which was unfenced and unprotected in any way. A death-trap for a eighteen-month-old little girl. He and Stanley worked until the light faded and they were out again early in the morning to complete the job and that horrifying drop to the basement was fenced.

A week later our new dog arrived. We had planned for a puppy but then we heard of Jumbo, a big gentle four-year-old labrador-German-shepherd cross who needed a new home because his owners were emigrating. Although he wasn't used to children and must have been upset by the change in his life, he never showed it. He became a wonderful family dog and shared our lives for the next eleven years. Our little black cat Teddy and he accepted each other at once and became good friends.

But not poor old Puss who hated and feared him on sight, for dogs had played no part in her life. We tried to introduce them gently but she couldn't tolerate him at all. One unfortunate day I opened the back door to let Jumbo out as Puss, unknown to me, was coming up the long flight of steps from the yard. When he appeared she ran, as usual, and that time he chased her. We never saw her again although we searched for her day after day. The old stables were some distance from the house and thinking that she might be living there we left food for her but it was rarely touched. Some months later Stanley found a litter of three dead kittens, two of them deformed. It was a sad end for Puss and upset me greatly.

The day of Stanley's Institution was approaching and in the rectory the phone rang constantly. Everyone in the parish, it seemed, needed him for something. Our very first car, a green Morris Minor, had been delivered and Stanley's parents had come from Sligo.

The fourth of September was a perfect late summer's day, with the heather-covered Wicklow mountains glowing deep purple in the sunshine. That evening we drove the one and a half miles from Annamoe and turned up the steep lane from the main road to Derralossary Church. We were early but people were already arriving. From the tiny hall opposite came the clink of china as the women of the parish prepared supper. We walked through the graveyard and into the ancient building filled with the scent of flowers and the glow of candle-light, for it was a church with no electricity. We opened the door of a horse-box pew and as Stanley's parents and I took our seats the last rays of the sun shone through the plain glass windows. The church was filling fast. People had come from all over the parish, from Glendalough to Calary, by car, bus, bicycle and even tractor, for the service that was to mark the beginning of a new ministry. Our friends from Clontarf were there too. The harmonium played the opening notes of the first hymn, the clergy processed up the aisle and the Institution service began.

That evening Archbishop Simms conferred upon Stanley 'The care and government of the souls of the parishioners of the United Parishes of Derralossary and Calary this 4th day of September in the year of our Lord one thousand nine hundred and fifty seven.' As we left the church a great orange moon had risen. Cars were parked all along the narrow lane and leaning against the walls of the parish hall were dozens of well-worn and much used bicycles. Inside, a long trestle table, covered by a starched white linen cloth, was laden with sandwiches, scones, sausage-rolls and cakes. Strong hot tea was poured from enormous pots into white delph cups and Stanley and I moved through the crowd in that tiny packed hall meeting the parishioners. The women all wore hats, for no one, in those days, would appear in church without one, the men sombre, dark formal suits. The evening ended and as we returned to the rectory the three street lights of Annamoe village couldn't compete with the full moon.

The next day my parents went home to Dalkey, my mother to make curtains for the large rectory windows. Stanley's parents stayed for a week and then they too went home. Now we were on our own.

That afternoon, as Stanley left the house to visit his parish, Judith and I got ready for our first walk. In Clontarf I had pushed her out every day in her pram; I would do the same in Annamoe. The Georgian rectory had two acres of garden and twenty-nine acres of land. A parishioner leased the land from the parish and grazed bullocks there. The avenue, beyond the garden gate, was over a quarter of a mile long through the unfenced land where the bullocks roamed freely. I left the house, with Judith sitting happily in her pram, and Jumbo trotting beside us. I opened and closed the wooden gate from the garden and now we had a long walk through that unfenced land. Near by was a huge monkey-puzzle-tree, its prickly foliage dark in the sunshine, and I thought how strange it was to see it, a native of Chile, growing in the middle of an Irish meadow. On we went and the only sound was of the river and the wind in the tree-tops. Then I heard something else. To our left was a steep hill to the upper pastures and from that direction came the thunder of hooves.

I watched in horror as over the brow of the hill streamed sixteen huge bullocks at full gallop, heading straight for pram, dog and me. Kicking and bucking they wheeled, at the very last moment, crossing the avenue only yards from where we stood, to disappear past the monkey-puzzle in the direction of the river. I ran in sheer terror. The pram rattled and banged over the stones all the way to the outer gate. With shaking fingers I opened and closed it behind me. My legs were weak with fright and the dog was terrified too. But Judith was delighted. 'More run,' she said clapping her hands with pleasure.

When Jumbo and I had recovered we continued our walk over the bridge and up the road towards Tomriland. We walked for a mile or two but we met no one and not one car passed us. I hardly noticed, for my thoughts were centred on the journey home back through the rectory grounds. At last we turned and retraced our steps. As we came to the bend in the road I could see the rectory across the valley on the far side of the river. Over the bridge, turn left through the trees – and standing just inside the rectory gate were the bullocks. There was no way home except past them.

'Lovey buggeds,' Judith said. Silently I called them something else.

As we approached the gate Jumbo stopped, afraid to go

further. I leaned over the top bar waving my arms and shouting. The bullocks looked at me with large, limpid eyes. Inside the gate was a derelict gate lodge and from its dark interior more bullocks appeared. Picking up a stone I threw it, and then another and another. I was way off the mark but bit by bit I began to find my target. Jumbo, thinking it was a game, barked loudly. Startled, the bullocks took off in a mad stampede along the avenue. It was now or never. I had to do it. Opening the gate I trundled the pram through. Closing it behind me, I ran. Expecting those large animals round every corner, that quarter of a mile to the house, some of it uphill, seemed endless. I got there at last with not a bullock in sight.

A few days later Stanley spoke to the farmer who owned them. 'They're a wild lot,' he said, 'I'll be taking them off the land soon.' He did take them off but it wasn't long before another batch arrived.

Annamoe means the Ford of the Cows. To me, considering my initiation to life there, the Ford of the Bullocks would have been more apt.

5

Between the Mountains and the Sea

Stanley's parish of Derralossary and Calary in County Wicklow was eleven miles from the sea and covered an area of 150 square miles of mountains, lakes and wooded valleys, stretching from Calary bog in the north to Glendalough seventeen miles south. The little church of Calary, built in 1834, was close to the Sugarloaf and Djouce mountains where thousands of sheep grazed the slopes. It was in this area that the greatest number of parishioners lived on isolated farms. Only twenty miles from Dublin but 800 feet above sea level, the weather in winter is harsh, with bitter winds whipping across the flat lands bringing snow to the bogs and mountains. Life on those isolated farms was hard then with few cars or telephones, no TVs and not many creature comforts. Calary farmers, their wives and families had to be tough to survive that environment.

There were, however, some large properties in this area and one of them was Tittour, the farm owned by Travers Nuttall. The big stone house, a few miles from Calary Church, was approached by a long descending avenue and surrounded by lawns and trees. Inside there were paintings by Jack Yeats, George Russell (AE) and Sarah Purser, who was related to the family; one very large Yeats picture hung in the enormous stone-flagged kitchen. It was a home with teenage children and the atmosphere was warm and welcoming. Travers had a brother, Freeman, who lived at Culleenamore in County Sligo. One day Stanley told Travers that he and I did our courting in the sand-hills at Culleenamore. With a twinkle in his eye he replied, 'Then you were trespassing on my property, for I own all that land.'

A few miles north of Roundwood at Knockraheen, Frank and Stella Warren lived and trained race-horses. One afternoon, when we were there on a visit, a gentle mare was led out for me to ride. I didn't think I aquitted myself too well but afterwards I was invited to 'ride out' at 7 am any morning when they exercised the horses. I would have loved to have accepted the invitation but I knew that my horsemanship wasn't up to that, so I didn't take up the offer. Each August Frank showed horses at the Royal Dublin Society's annual show at Ballsbridge, and long after we had left Annamoe, and he and Stella had moved to Kilnamanagh in County Wexford, I would see him there, still winning prizes.

But not all the parishioners in the Calary parish farmed. Camille Souter, who has since become a very well-known painter, lived with her husband and children in a cottage not far from the Sugarloaf. Dr Collis, the famous paediatrician, had a house at Bow Island which he used for holidays; after he died his widow and son continued to live there, and one winter, when the snow was so deep on Calary bog that the farm animals had to be fed with hay dropped from a helicopter, they had to be air-lifted to safety.

The centre of Stanley's parish was near Roundwood at Derralossary, which means the Oak Grove of the Flame. The church, built on an ancient druid site, had horse-box pews and was lit by 120 candles. High up overlooking the valley, with the mountains in the distance, it was a wild and windy spot in winter. The parishioners here were few in number and widely scattered and included the Barton family of Glendalough House.

The third church in the parish, St John's, stood in a small wood above the village of Laragh, beside Laragh Castle where the sculptors Imogen and Ian Stuart (son of the writer Francis) lived with their children for some years when we were there. The parishioners in this parish were mostly elderly and well-to-do and came from the surrounding valleys of Glendasan, Glendalough and the Vale of Clara.

Glendalough means the Valley of the Two Lakes and in the sixth century there was a great monastic city there, founded by Saint Kevin, of more than 3,000 people. Within the city there were seven churches, cells for the monks, halls for study, libraries, workshops, houses for composing and copying manuscripts, all surrounded by farms, fields and woods. It became a centre in the religious world of Europe, with many scholars travelling there to study, and it was also a place of pilgrimage. But trials beset the community in the shape of plunderings and burnings by the Vikings and the Normans. The round tower, 31 metres high and near the entrance gate, was used as a watch-tower and as a safe place for both humans and the city treasures. Saint Kevin lived at the monastic city but it is thought that he spent much time in a small cave in the sheer rock face above the waters of the Upper Lake. The Lower Lake, beside the city, is the smaller of the two and is linked to the Upper Lake by the Glenale River.

Glendalough is beautiful and a popular place with tourists but the Upper Lake is strange and mysterious, with dark, sombre, overhanging cliffs. The wind funnels down between the mountains and storms come suddenly; there have been many tragedies there over the years. During our time in Annamoe we rarely saw Glendalough in all its beauty for the valley, deep in the mountains, is often covered with mist. But one winter's day as we walked by the Lower Lake, the air crackling with cold, it was magical. Passing through the ruins of the monastic city we crossed the little bridge over the Glenale River where dragon-flies hover in summer. The path between the trees was white with frost, the bushes spangled with silver. Across the valley someone was chopping wood and the sound carried sharply on the icy air. Suddenly, from nowhere it seemed, a pure white labrador dog appeared. Seeing us, he hesitated, before slipping between the trees to disappear as swiftly and silently as he had come. Was it a real dog, we wondered, or some spirit of the valley?

Annamoe, twenty-seven miles from Dublin and five from
Glendalough, was to become the centre of our world for the
next five and a half years. In the middle of the village,
behind the post-office, were the entrance gates to
Glendalough House, home of the Barton family. A long tree-
lined avenue led to sweeping lawns which stretched beyond
the porticoed front door. Behind this Victorian-gothic
structure sprawled the older part of the house with its virginia
creeper covered walls, overlooking rose-beds and more
spacious lawns. At the east side there were extensive water
gardens with calm pools, running rivulets, tumbling minature
waterfalls, ferns and exotic plants.

Bob Barton farmed the large estate and gave employment
to much of Annamoe village. When we first met him he was
already elderly, a slight grey-haired man dressed in fawn
tweeds. When young he was elected Sinn Fein MP for west
Wicklow and became Minister for Agriculture in the first
Dail. He was arrested and imprisoned in Mountjoy but
managed to escape in the same year; he enjoyed telling
Stanley that he left a note for the Governor saying that he
couldn't stay any longer as he wasn't satisfied with the
service. He founded the National Bank before being
rearrested and sentenced to three years penal servitude. He
was one of the signatories of the Anglo-Irish Treaty in 1921,
and was appointed Minister for Economic Affairs in the
second Dail a year later. Late in life he had married his
widowed cousin Rachel from Boston. I found him a rather
austere, remote man but he was kind to us. His niece, on
holiday from England, once called at the rectory and reported
back to him that we had little furniture and that Stanley had
no study desk, which was true. A few days later a large, old-
fashioned roll-top desk was delivered to us from Glendalough
House. Each Christmas he gave Stanley a present of a battery
or a new tyre for his car.

Bob Barton was related to the Childers family; the mother
of Erskine Childers senior was Anna Barton. When both she

and her husband Robert died, their children moved to Annamoe to be cared for and grow up with their five Barton cousins at Glendalough House. They spent a happy childhood there and Erskine developed a great love for the surrounding mountains, valleys, lakes and rivers. Slim and of middle height, he was strong and athletic and enjoyed walking vast distances over the Wicklow hills. In the quiet and solitude of the large estate at Glendalough House he was able to read, write and study without any distractions. He learned much from the local people and was interested to hear them arguing about the Land War and Parnell. His book, *The Riddle of the Sands*, a thriller and an adventure story, brought him fame and it sold millions of copies. But the greatest influence on his life was to be his future wife, Molly Osgood. They became engaged only six weeks after they met and were married three months later. Her father's wedding-present to them was the yacht *Asgard* which was built by one of the world's best yacht designers, a Norwegian. Later the *Asgard* became famous when it was used to bring guns and ammunition to Ireland for the Irish Volunteers. It was Molly who was at the helm when they landed fire-arms at Howth in 1914. Seven years later Erskine was secretary of the delegation led by Michael Collins and Arthur Griffith, which went to London to negotiate with the British Government.

Erskine Childers was to die tragically in one of the most senseless incidents of the Irish Civil War (1922-1924). The Anglo-Irish Treaty of December 1921 had resulted in the setting up of the Irish Free State for twenty-six of Ireland's counties. It was opposed by a number of IRA leaders and civil war followed in June 1922. Guerilla warfare was conducted by the anti-Treaty forces and so the new Provisional Government introduced, in October, the Army Emergency Powers which made carrying arms an offence, the punishment for which could be death. The following month Childers was arrested and found to be in 'unauthorised possession' of a pistol. In spite of the fact that he was not a combat officer and that the death sentence was not mandatory, he was executed by firing-squad, along with four Republican soldiers, on 24 November. A previous rector of Annamoe, the Rev Edward Waller, had been a great friend of his, and it was he whom Erskine asked to attend the execution in Beggars' Bush barrracks in Dublin. Ironically, the tiny pearl-handled pistol that caused his death had been a present from Michael Collins

When we moved to Annamoe his widow Molly, who was elderly and bedridden, lived at Glendalough House with the Bartons. She suffered from bad arthritis and her room temperature had to be kept so high that the heat was almost unbearable. Beside her bed was a large framed photograph of her late husband, flanked always by fresh flowers. Stanley enjoyed his visits to Mrs Childers for she had a keen sense of humour and loved telling him stories of things that had amused her greatly. One Sunday in Derralossary Church the then rector preached a fiery sermon condemning the evils of luxurious living and of wallowing in thick carpets. As she looked at the small congregation of farmers and their wives, she wondered at whom the sermon was directed. Deciding that it must be at her own family, she later challenged the rector. 'Oh no,' he replied. 'I got *that* sermon from a book.' She enjoyed reading and gave Stanley a copy of *A City Without Walls*, an anthology of world-famous authors compiled by her mother, Margaret Cushing Osgood. When Stanley lent her one of the series of books called *Design in Nature* by his great uncle, Professor James Bell Pettigrew, she was so impressed that she wrote him a long letter saying how much she had enjoyed it.

Her son, also Erskine, his wife Rita and their daughter Nessa came to visit her at Glendalough House every August and they usually invited us and the children for tea. Nessa had a wonderful collection of dolls from around the world which Judith looked at with longing.

When Molly Childers died, Stanley was asked to conduct

the funeral and burial service. Standing by the graveside in the Republican Plot in Glasnevin Cemetery in Dublin were three men who would become Presidents of Ireland.

We were to meet Erskine Childers again some years after we left Annamoe. He was campaigning for the presidency of Ireland and asked Stanley to arrange a meeting for him in Wicklow rectory with some of the prominent people in the town. The campaign bus parked on the main road while he and his entourage walked up the avenue to the house but it was only a whistle-stop, for within minutes they were on their way again. When he was elected President, we were invited to his inaugural reception in Dublin Castle. It was a very grand affair with the guests being greeted at the top of the sweeping staircase by the Taoiseach, Liam Cosgrove, and his wife, before going into the banqueting hall where we were received by the new President and Mrs Childers. Sadly. his presidency was tragically short for he died eighteen months later; he was buried at Derralossary. His younger brother, Bobby, who had a distinguished career in publishing in England, lived in a wing of Glendalough House for many years until his death as a very old man in 1997. The house and estate have now changed hands, ending many years of ownership and occupancy by the Barton and Childers families.

Down the hill and over the bridge was Annaglen, home of the Glendinnings. Angus, with his bushy eyebrows, military moustache and fawn duffle-coat, looked every inch the colonel that he was. His wife Sybil was warm, motherly and kind. Ian, their only child, was a major in the British army. Their thatched cottage with its beautiful garden, at the bend where the Dublin, Glendalough and Wicklow roads meet, was the sunniest and busiest corner in Annamoe. Everyone stopped there to chat for the Glendinnings were hospitable people. Both were early risers and each morning, when the village was barely stirring, Angus walked up the hill to buy his *Irish Times*. Then, sitting in their winter garden conservatory, amongst the flowers and the pot plants, he read it from cover to cover. Their garden ran down to the river and they kept geese. In the morning, when the geese were let out of their barn, they would waddle noisily along the banks to disappear down river. In the late afternoon we often heard Sybil call, 'Dilly, Dilly,' as they went home.

The Glendinnings loved children and during our years in Annamoe they gave wonderful parties for the sons and daughters of their many friends, with some of the small guests being ferried in from quite a distance away. One hot summer's day when the new goose pond was finished, but not yet in use, it was christened with a swimming party. Angus, wearing an old-fashioned black bathing-suit, splashed and cavorted in the water with the children until Sybil called everyone to tea on the lawn. There were adult parties at Annaglen too. Sometimes, when we had no baby-sitter, Stanley would stay at home while Angus collected me for dinner and ran me home afterwards. I enjoyed those evenings out and Sybil's excellent cooking. We greatly appreciated their kindness to us during our time in Annamoe.

Patsy was our postman. His home, opposite Annaglen, had no neat lawns or brightly coloured flowers but its grey walls gave shelter to his sheep. Every morning, six days a week, he cycled up the avenue to the rectory to deliver our post and his visit was the highlight of the day. 'Postie's coming,' the children would call excitedly, running to the front door to take the letters. Not once in five and a half years did Patsy let us down. In pouring rain and gale force wind he came and when the snow was too deep for him to cycle he trudged on foot, bag over his shoulder, the half mile from the village. He must have cycled great distances on his daily round for many of the houses had long avenues but we never heard him complain; he always had a smile and a kind word for everyone.

Beyond the Glendinnings' cottage the road to Wicklow takes a short, sharp bend to the right. Below, in the river valley, is the rectory while ahead, on a high hill backed by dark trees and approached by a long steep avenue, the grey stone house of Castlekevin rises starkly. Once owned by the O'Tooles, Castlekevin was the centre of rebel activity in the thirteenth century and again in the year 1800 when Andrew Thomas, a native of Drummin near Annamoe, was shot and killed for his rebel activities. At the end of the last century Castlekevin was owned by the Fitzells but, following evictions, the house was boycotted. The family left and the property lay vacant. It was rented out for the summer months, and the family of playwright John Millington Synge spent many holidays there. The Synges were nervous at first of staying in a boycotted house so sometimes in the evenings two constables would come up the avenue and walk round the outbuildings to see that all was well. Only once was there any unpleasantness. The stableman had taken their horse to the forge but the blacksmith, claiming that the man had been involved in the evictions, refused to shoe it. If a member of the Synge family brought the horse to the forge personally, the blacksmith said he would be quite willing to do the job. This they did and the situation was happily resolved.

The views from the sloping lawns in front of Castlekevin down to the river, with the Barton estate and the mountains beyond, were spectacular, especially at sunset. As the sun sank behind Scar, sometimes through a veil of mist, the sky would turn deep red while the tips of the clouds were edged with gold. During our time in Annamoe Castlekevin was owned and farmed by an English couple but that house, with its unhappy history, has changed ownership many times.

Another house the Synge family sometimes rented was at Tomriland, two miles from Annamoe. It was here that Synge wrote *In the Shadow of the Glen*. 'I got more aid than any learning could give me,' he said, 'from a chink in the floor of the old house where I was staying, that let me hear what was being said by the servant girls in the kitchen.' Synge loved

County Wicklow with its wide open spaces, heather-covered hills and unfenced pasture where mountain sheep grazed. He and his brothers looked upon themselves as Wicklow men and one of them, Dr Sam, became rector of Annamoe after returning from the mission field in China. His daughter, Edith, called on us once at the rectory and over the years we got to know her well. She was fond of travelling and even as an old lady spent time abroad, sometimes in exotic places, each year. Another member of that family, a young man called Francis, came to see us often and became a good friend.

Beyond the main gates of Castlekevin, Willie and Kathleen Belton lived in a two-hundred-year-old farm-house. They kept geese, turkeys and ducks, and early in December, in our first year in the rectory, they told us that they would give us a turkey for Christmas, which they kindly did every year that we lived there.

Half a mile from the village, on the road to Dublin and overlooking the Avonmore River is Uplands, built by a cousin of the Synges; she had been brought up in England but returned to Ireland, on the death of her mother, to live amongst the Wicklow hills. The well-known Irish actor, Cyril Cusack, also lived there for a time.

This then was the parish that Stanley inherited in 1957. Its people and terraine, as diverse from one another as could possibly be imagined, were an immense challenge for a young man.

6
Ice on the Window Panes

That first winter in Annamoe, Judith and I were alone often, for as a new rector Stanley was in demand to preach and visit other parishes. September is the month of harvest festivals and hardly had we settled in after his Institution than he had to go to Delgany fifteen miles away. Judith was in bed and asleep when he left; I faced a long evening alone. As darkness fell I looked out of the curtainless windows but there was no comforting glow outside from street light or houses. It was very black and the silence was deep. I sat by the fire knitting while Jumbo, with Teddy between his paws, dozed on the hearth-rug. I put on the radio but not for long, for even with the sitting-room door open it was hard to hear if Judith, far upstairs, cried. I tried to read and an hour or two passed. I made a cup of tea and as I drank it by the fire, Jumbo gave a low menacing growl. His hackles rose as he leaped to his feet, barking wildly. He raced to the window and then into the hall to the front door. He was very angry as he ran his nose along the bottom of the door in a snuffling growl. *Who* was outside I wondered? The front door was heavy and strong but one kick would have knocked the flimsy back door flat.

The rest of the evening crawled by. I jumped at every sound and when ten o'clock came I knew that I was really alone, cut off from the outside world, for that was the hour when the exchange (in Wicklow) disconnected our telephone for the night. At half past ten Judith wakened. This had become a nightly occurrence. In Clontarf, with the traffic roaring past, she had slept soundly but in the quietness of the countryside she wakened often. As I comforted her,

Jumbo barked again. To my immense relief it was Stanley coming home.

I had never lived in a house as old as the rectory and when darkness fell I was nervous, not only of what was outside the house but of what might be *inside* too. Could the house have a ghost? Was it haunted? Old houses creak and groan a lot and I was conscious of every sound. Sometimes I would stand on the landing upstairs listening to the wind moaning through the trees and the tapping and scratching of branches on the window panes. However, as time passed, I felt that there was nothing to fear in Annamoe rectory, although I did once hear something in that two-hundred-year-old house that I couldn't explain. Luckily, that evening I was not alone.

The days were growing shorter with a chill in the air. Often a damp mist rose from the river, drifting over the fields and woods, blotting out the landscape. The leaves had turned and the ground under our feet was a carpet of brown, red, russet and gold. It was so quiet that we could hear the leaves as they left the branches and fluttered to the ground. The bullocks had gone so we could walk in safety. In a tall tree near the outer gate lived a red squirrel. We saw him often, swinging through the branches or scurrying up the rough bark, his bushy tail waving. His home was in a cavity high above our heads and our daily walk had to include a visit to 'Squirl'. Beyond the squirrel tree was the derelict gate lodge and then, another hundred yards, the bridge and the road.

Sometimes we made it up the hill to the village shop owned by Joe, a parishioner, crowded when four people were inside. This was the hub of the whole village. As you entered, a bell above the door rang loudly and all eyes turned in your direction. Joe, red-faced and wearing a brown dust-coat, stood behind the counter taking orders, breathing heavily as he removed groceries from the shelves. A pencil stub lay on the counter with a stack of notebooks close by, for if you had an account you had a notebook. Slowly and laboriously every item bought was written down and the total totted up. Each day Stanley collected our milk there but even for one item you had to wait your turn. It was a slow business shopping at Joe's. The shelves were crowded with tea, sugar, tins of corned beef, baked beans, carbolic soap, matches and bundles of white candles. Butter and fatty rashers, sliced thick, stood beside the scales ready to be weighed. Joe was meticulous at that, changing the heavy brass weights often until he had the amount just right. Occasionally we asked for something that was not on his shelves. Fixing us with an outraged stare he would say severely, 'I don't stock that. There's no call for it.'

Each week we bought a packet of Marietta and some USA biscuits. Taking a white paper bag from beneath the counter, he would open the glass-fronted tin and carefully count out the USA assortment. Two of everything went into the bag, except for the chocolate biscuits; only one of those per customer was the rule. Once, after our son John was born, Stanley asked, 'Any chance of a second chocolate biscuit for my two children?' Joe looked at him over his glasses, breathing hard. 'If I give *you* two,' he said, 'what will I give my other customers?' Stanley never asked again. Accounts had to be settled promptly, no extra credit was allowed. In those days the Church of Ireland only paid their clergy every three months, and it was a long time to budget for. Sometimes Stanley had to ask Joe to wait a day or two until his stipend cheque arrived. Joe didn't approve of that even though, as a vestry member and a church warden of Derra-lossary, he knew exactly what Stanley's salary was.

Dusk came early on those late autumn afternoons and it was often falling as Judith and I made our way home after our walk. As I pushed the pram back up the avenue and through the garden gate I had to pass a dense high hedge, nearly as tall as the house. Beyond it was the large, cobbled yard and a dark wood of macrocarpa trees. Could anyone be lurking there? I wondered as pram and I took the last hundred yards to the front door at a gallop. I told my father of my fear and on his next visit, without saying a word to anyone, he cut the hedge down to shoulder height. Stanley wasn't pleased; the hedge had been ruined, he said, but I was happy

Slowly we had been putting the house in order. The curtains were finished. My mother had made them all on her hand-turned Singer sewing-machine and when they were hung, the house was transformed. Our bedroom seemed less enormous and the study looked almost furnished, with an old brown carpet on the floor and a large armchair belonging to my father. The second-hand stair carpet was down but we had no floor covering for the hall so we went to Dublin, my first trip there since we left Clontarf. Stanley had just learned to drive so the journey would be a test for him. Carefully he drove through Roundwood, over Calary bog and down the Long Hill to Kilmacanogue. We met little traffic, even on the road to Bray, and in Dublin we found a parking space with ease at St Stephen's Green. After much searching we found what we were looking for – Tintawn, a coconut matting, hard wearing and cheap.

One day, a week later, a motor-bike came roaring along the rectory avenue and, with much revving, pulled up outside the house. As I opened the front door and the rider approached, Judith clung to me in terror. Winding her arms tightly round my neck, her hot wet tears flowed over me. As the young man tried to tell me what he wanted his voice was completely drowned by Judith's loud crying. Shrugging his shoulders resignedly he left, wheeling his bike down to the garden gate before riding away. I never did discover what he had come for. One afternoon, shortly after that episode, Stanley took us to Glendalough to have a walk. The Royal Hotel was locked and shuttered as we drove past, the souvenir stall at the gate boarded up too, for the summer season was over. We drove to the Upper Lake, parked the car and began our walk. There was no one else about but we had only gone a few yards when, in the distance, we heard the sound of a motor-bike. Judith heard it too. We hoped that it wouldn't come our way but it noisily pulled up beside us.

Screams and sobs came from Judith as we retreated to the safety of the car which she refused to leave.

As we drove away Stanley had an idea. 'We'll go to Glenmalure,' he said. 'There's a small hotel in the valley where we might get a cup of tea.' The drive through the mountains past Lugnaquilla, Wicklow's highest peak, was beautiful in the autumn sunshine, but when we got there that hotel was closed too. Annamoe's three street lights shone feebly in the dusk as we drove through the village and home. As we turned down by the river to the rectory avenue my spirits were low, for at that hour in Clontarf Judith and I would have been returning from our afternoon walk with buses passing, shop windows brightly lit and the sound of voices. How long, I wondered, would it take me to get used to this new life? I was glad to hear Jumbo's welcoming bark as we opened the front door.

The following week invitations to afternoon tea-parties began to arrive. As the curate's wife in Clontarf I had been spared those and, not being sure of what to wear, I consulted my mother who could always be relied on in such matters. 'Play it safe,' she said. 'Wear your best suit (my wedding 'going away' suit), a hat and gloves.' I soon discovered that the suit and gloves were correct but that the hat wasn't necessary. As I dressed Judith for the first tea-party, in her white leggings and pale blue coat and tied a fluffy bonnet over her fair hair, I tried to prepare that shy little girl for the event. Over the next few weeks we were entertained many times and the pattern was always the same. On arrival, at four o'clock, four or five guests would be waiting in the drawing-room to meet us. At twenty past four we all sat down to tea in a chilly dining-room. A place was always laid for Judith and, at nineteen months, she was expected to sit up at the table. Tea was poured from a silver pot into fine china cups, the sandwiches were small and dainty, the scones served with home-made jam or honey. Judith, her large dining-room chair pulled up close beside me and a hot little hand holding one of mine tightly, would eat a rusk or a biscuit which I had brought with me. Afterwards, Stanley carefully picked up the soggy crumbs from the carpet. At a quarter past five the guests departed.

At one party Judith decided to explore. She trotted round the room as we made polite conversation. Stanley and I watched her closely for there were valuable objects everywhere but she touched nothing. Suddenly, from behind a large armchair, we heard her say, '*Oh dear, dear, dear,*' and we knew what had happened. A large puddle had formed on the parquet floor, missing the Persian carpet by inches, somehow almost completely bypassing her nappie and plastic pants. At that moment tea was announced. As we followed our unsuspecting hostess into the dining-room, Stanley deftly pushed the large armchair over the puddle.

The last tea-party we were invited to that first autumn took place in late November. There were fourteen guests and some of them, having travelled a distance, were in no hurry to leave. At six o'clock, which was Judith's bath, tea and bedtime, we were still seated at the long mahogany dining-room table. As she grew restless I tried to catch Stanley's eye but he was deep in conversation. Picking her up in my arms I walked to the top of the table and, seeing me coming, he stood up too. Our hostess looked at me coldly. 'What a shame to break up my party,' she said. 'I would have thought you could have stayed longer.'

Those formal tea-parties were kindly meant but with a small child they were an ordeal. No allowance at all was made for her; she was expected to be good and she was, for not once did she cry or make a fuss. But it was a great relief when they came to an end. I had an added reason for feeling that way for I was expecting another baby.

The golden days of autumn were over, the trees showed bare against the winter sky and the river, swollen by endless rain, was sullen and grey. The new Tintawn matting now covered the hall floor and although we still hadn't much furniture, on every wall pictures that Stanley had painted glowed with colour. Christmas was approaching. We brought holly in from the woods and a small tree which we put in a corner of the sitting-room. Judith helped me to decorate it. 'Pretty,' she said as she handed me the strands of silver tinsel and the golden star for the top.

On Christmas Eve Stanley had to go out. As he left, Judith and I were putting the finishing touches to our tree. Jumbo was sitting at one of the tall windows looking out. Suddenly, he gave a growl. A man was standing just inside the garden gate looking at the house. Slowly, he began to walk up the avenue but instead of coming to the front door, he disappeared into the cobbled yard at the back. 'Who was he?' I wondered for no one except Sybil and Angus walked to the rectory – everyone else came by car or bike. I hurried to the study window and stood in the shadow of the curtains to watch. In the yard below the man, dressed in a long black coat, stopped to stare up at the three storeys of the house. 'The back door!' I thought in panic. 'It's unlocked.' As I turned the key, heavy footsteps sounded, coming up the flight of steps from the yard. Jumbo heard them too and began to bark. A knock sounded and a white expressionless face looked in through the kitchen window. The man gestured to me to open the door. 'I can't open it,' I shouted above the noise of Jumbo's barking. 'The dog will get out.' The man gestured again.

Really frightened now, in desperation I began a charade. I pretended the house was full of people. 'Stanley,' I called loudly, 'someone wants you.' Then I called to my father and after that to my mother. Judith, delighted with the game, joined in. All the time the man watched me through the window. 'Everyone's busy,' I shouted to him at last and I left the kitchen. Still the man knocked, louder now. I went to the study and looked at the telephone but there was no one I could ring; Sybil and Angus had no phone and neither had anyone else in the village. At last the man left, walking quickly through the yard and out through the garden gate, leaving it open behind him. From the sitting-room window I watched him disappear down the avenue.

Six months later Stanley's predecessor in Annamoe called to see us. As he was leaving he asked, 'Did a young fellow call on you last Christmas Eve? We used to give him a few bob, for the poor chap's deaf and dumb.'

Christmas was over and Annamoe was in the grip of winter. When we awoke in the mornings ice covered the inside of our bedroom windows. The wind whistled through the badly fitting frames and we stuffed the gaps with newspapers and old jumpers to keep out the draughts. On a fine morning Judith slept outside in her pram for an hour or so. When she awoke she would sit up, rosy-cheeked, to watch the world go by – the clouds in the sky, the birds flying, the branches of the trees waving. Once it began to snow and she held out her hands to catch the flakes. When she grew lonely she would call loudly, 'Mum-mee-eee,' and I would hurry out to bring her into the house. Often it felt colder inside than it did outside, for the temperature in the hall was only two degrees above freezing-point and when Judith played there I dressed her in her outdoor clothes. For Christmas we gave her a doll's pram, a very basic affair made of red, painted wood. Now on our daily walk her own big pram stayed at home and she pushed the little red one down the avenue with her doll and panda tucked in. We travelled slowly then.

On winter evenings I had company now, for the little field-mice, great armies of them, or so it seemed, came marching into the house to find warmth. I liked to hear them scuttling about. In our Clontarf flat we had mice and Stanley set a trap. To my horror I found a tiny one caught, shaking and bleeding but still alive. I released him, nursed him back to health and let him go free. Stanley set a trap in Annamoe rectory too and one morning we found a long tail caught but no mouse. We never set that kind of trap again. We tried another method. Putting some cheese into a milk bottle, we placed it in an area which the mice frequented. Tipping the bottle at an angle, with the food at the lower end so that the mice could run in but not out again, we checked it often to make sure that any creatures caught wouldn't suffocate. It worked! One winter we caught thirty-two mice which we set free outside. We had a strong suspicion, however, that they all came inside again, for the number in the house never seemed to decrease.

Every day Stanley cut logs from fallen tree branches in the rectory grounds and brought them into the sitting-room for the fire. Sometimes the wood was good but at other times it sizzled and spat, with dribbles of moisture running down the logs and on to the hearth. Then we added coal to help it to burn.

One afternoon I sat by the fire knitting while Judith played beside me. That day we had no walk, for another lorry load of bullocks had arrived. We could hear them bellowing out in the fields as they galloped around while Jumbo barked and barked at their noise but now he was quiet, asleep on the hearth-rug. The wood for the fire was bad that day and the room was growing cold. I reached for the coal-bucket. It was empty. Now I had a journey to make and I didn't relish the thought. Walking through the hall I opened the door to the basement and closed the child safety gate at the top of the long flight of stairs. It was almost dark down there for the daylight was fading. I pressed the light switch and the low-watt bulb dimly lit up the dusty corners and the open doors to the many rooms below. Judith and Jumbo watched as I carefully descended the rickety staircase. A smell of dampness rose to meet me. I crossed the stone passage to the old kitchen and pressed another light switch. It was as cold as a morgue and my footsteps echoed as I crossed the enormous room where large meat-hooks hung menacingly from the ceiling. In the furthest corner was a heavy door, journey's end. Pulling it open, I put on yet another light, which lit up a dark cavern with a small pile of coal against one wall. Picking up the shovel I flung coal into the bucket, switched off the light, banged the door closed and fled. Judith and Jumbo were patiently waiting for me at the top of the basement stairs as I closed the door to the underworld behind me.

Kathleen was coming on a visit. I hadn't seen her since my wedding-day when she and Ethne were my bridesmaids. Kathleen and I had grown up together and at school we were 'best friends'; but our ways parted when she went to London to become a nurse. Now she was coming to Annamoe to meet her god-daughter Judith, and to say good-bye to us, for she was emigrating to Canada. I wanted to impress her with my cooking so I got out my school recipe-books, large maroon hard-backed exercise books with 'Belfast Royal Academy, Domestic Science Dept, Vera Brownell' written on the front cover. As I leafed through the pages I relived those cookery classes. Everything was costed in pre-decimal currency: shah biscuits 7d a batch; sponge-cake, beaten with a wooden spoon until your arm cried out with pain, 11d; Russian fish-pie, made with rough puff pastry, which took hours to make, for it had to be folded and rolled many times, 1s 2d. Plum-pudding was expensive at 2s 10d and included grated carrot, chopped apples and a tablespoon of marmalade – if we could get it – for in those years, after the war, almost everything was in short supply. Under the heading *Housewifery* we took notes, with diagrams, on the water supply (we knew all about S bends!). There were pages and pages on ranges, electric and gas cookers, the digestive system, hygiene, constipation and much, much more. Someone was determined to make us good and competent housewives.

As I closed my old recipe-books I hoped my cooking for Kathleen wouldn't be the disaster that my beef stew was when Anne came to stay with us in Clontarf. She too was a school friend and we had all endured together the agonies of learning French seams, run and fells, feather stitching and button-holes. We had giggled as we sewed 'our garments', ill-fitting, shapeless creations made by hand, with all irregular stitches ripped out and worked again. For Anne's visit I made my beef stew carefully with plenty of juicy carrots and nice firm onions. As I put it in the oven I worried about leaving the gas cooker on in the empty flat when I went to the station to meet her so I turned the heat low. One hour later we were back. 'I've made a stew,' I told her with pride, as I opened the oven door and removed the casserole lid. A grey congealed mass met my eyes; the stew hadn't even begun to cook. When we finally ate it, an hour or so later, it was still pretty raw.

Kathleen stayed with us in Annamoe for four days. I've forgotten what I cooked for her but I think it must have been reasonably successful. I missed her greatly when she left; I didn't know then that it would be thirty-five years before we would meet again.

It was March. Judith was going to be two years old and my parents had come for the big event. At the birthday tea they helped her to blow out the candles but she wouldn't eat any of her cake. The next morning, Sunday, we wakened to a white world for snow had come in the night. On the large gravel sweep in front of the house and the avenue down to the garden gate it was deep – and Stanley had services to take. He began to dig. By nine am he had reached the gate but outside, on the main avenue, the snow was deeper still. He dug until eleven o'clock when, exhausted, he admitted defeat. In the afternoon we heard a tractor on the avenue; the farmer was bringing hay to his bullocks but he didn't come near us at the house. Judith had never seen deep snow before and she looked in wonder at the white world outside, all the familiar landmarks gone. The tree branches were heavy laden and on top of each fence post was a perfect snowball. Animal tracks showed plainly in the whiteness, evidence of the inhabitants of another world, rarely seen. We dressed Judith warmly, put on her gum boots and out she went with Stanley and my father to built a snowman. Jumbo too had never seen snow before and he barked excitedly as he galloped in circles. My mother and I watched from the porch, for at six months pregnant I didn't want to risk falling. Across the river we could hear voices and laughter as people tobogganed.

That first fall lasted a week and then my parents went home. But soon the snow was back and that time it stayed much longer. No milk, post or newspapers came to the village for days and only Sybil and Angus trudged through the drifts to visit us. We saw no one else. Our isolation was complete.

7

The Call of the Cuckoo

In Annamoe the winter is long but at last, that first year, we wakened one morning to the drip, drip of water from the roof. The thaw had begun. The ice and snow were gone as suddenly as they had come, and soft breezes replaced the winter gales. We removed the sodden newspapers and old jumpers from the gaps in the window frames and opened the windows wide. Spring had come. All through the rectory fields, along the avenue and down by the river, daffodils bloomed. We gathered great armfuls of them and brought them into the house. Every day there was a new miracle as the tree buds opened and tiny green leaves unfurled and a carpet of bluebells replaced the daffodils. Across the valley, Ballenacorbeg hill was golden with gorse, its nutty perfume wafting on the breeze. The air was filled with bird song and the cuckoo called in sunshine and in rain, even through the night. On those spring mornings the first streaks of light had barely appeared in the sky when the dawn chorus began. Often it was the blackbird who sounded the first rich piping notes, to be joined, minutes later, by sparrow, robin, thrush and wren. In the tall trees, across the fields, the rooks cawed sleepily. From the hedgerows other birds joined in and soon the air was filled with wonderful liquid singing. Another day had begun.

On those beautiful spring evenings, as the long day drew to a close and the sun sank behind the hills, it was a never to be forgotten experience to stand outside in the rectory garden. As the moon rose over the tree-tops, turning the fields and woods silver white, bats swooped past. Beyond the fence the dark bodies of the bullocks moved like shadows over the

meadow and the sound of their rough tongues tearing the
long grass was loud in the quiet air. I often wondered what
was going on out there in nature's secret world of the night.
Was there a fox crossing the field on a well-worn track,
pausing, ears pricked, as our human smell reached him? Our
friend the squirrel, where did he go on moonlit nights? Were
there badgers in the wood, turning the earth with their
strong noses and claws, searching for beetles and grubs?
Badgers are shy secretive nocturnal animals, only emerging
from their setts, labyrinths of dark underground tunnels and
sleeping chambers, by night. But one evening as dusk began
to fall we heard the sound of ferocious growling and snapping
just yards from the house. We opened the back door and
there were two very large badgers fighting. They were so
preoccupied that they didn't notice us until the dog barked.
Then, breaking suddenly, they ambled off in opposite
directions to disappear into the gathering darkness.

My first encounter with a fox was extraordinary. As I sat
outside in the summer sunshine, a young vixen slipped
through the hedge and walked slowly towards me. Pausing to
smell a bed of mint, she stared intently down the garden,
probably looking for our dog. I held my breath as she came
closer. Then, to my astonishment, her cold, wet nose touched
my bare toe. I moved slightly and she sprang, cat-like, away.
Her rich red coat gleamed in the sunshine as she turned to
look at me. We eyed one another and I could see plainly the
white muzzle below the mask and her tiny ears flicking
backwards and forwards. Suddenly, she was gone. Was she as
amazed by her close encounter with a human as I was by
mine with a fox?

With the arrival of the swallows, friends and acquaintances
came to Annamoe to see us. 'How lucky you are,' they said,
'to live in such a beautiful place.' Picnickers came too, people
we didn't know at all, who opened the outer gate, drove
through, and sometimes left their litter behind and the gate
open when they departed. Often Stanley had to ask them to

move their cars to let him drive past. 'This is private property,' he said once. 'Is it?' came the answer and no one budged.

It was that first spring in Annamoe, at a Mothers' Union meeting, that my 'career' in public speaking began, Mary Sumner, the founder of the Mothers' Union, was a clergyman's wife in a remote Hampshire country parish in England. Feeling that women would benefit by meeting together regularly to chat and share their family problems, she invited them to the vicarage. That was in the year 1876 and from those small beginnings the Mothers' Union, now a worldwide organization, sprang. Although it was founded by the Anglican Church, women of all dominations, married and unmarried, may join. Men too are welcome. The Mothers' Union is specially concerned with all that strengthens and preserves marriage and Christian family life. In Ireland most parishes have a branch, and our monthly meetings took place in the tiny parochial hall at Derralossary. The evening began with prayer and a bible reading and sometimes we had a visiting speaker, but usually we, the members, made our own entertainment. I enjoyed those meetings and the chance to see and chat with the other women in our scattered parish. Mrs Wynne of Glendalough, our president, called at the rectory to see me. 'My dear,' she said, 'we would like you to read the lesson at our next meeting.' I was horrified, for I had never read in public before. But Mrs Wynne was adamant that, as the rector's wife, it was something I was *expected* to do.

The passage I had to read was short and not difficult but I practised and practised. I read it to Stanley and to Judith and to the dog and to the cat until I knew it by heart. I went to that meeting with clammy hands and a churning stomach. The room was cold, warmed only by a small oil-heater, but when I stood up to read my whole body was suffused with heat. As I finished and, with tremendous relief, sat down again, Mrs Wynne gave me a gentle approving smile. Over

First white Christmas –
Judith and Stanley

Summer in Annamoe –
Judith and me

Stanley's parents, Keeble and Kathleen,
with Judith and one-year-old John

Left: I'm holding John at his first birthday party, Judith seems determined to hold on to her three friends

Right: Judith and Flufty, one of the two rabbits the children had – until they decided to leave us for a life of their own.
Below: The canoe Stanley made from cardboard boxes, which was big enough for both Judith and John to fit into. With ropes over his shoulders he pulled them across the rectory lawn as they paddled 'up the Amazon'

Above: John and Judith with Jumbo, first of many family friends
Below: John and his 'fleet'

Top: Judith and John
Above: Judith and me in the rectory grounds

Left: Our friend Jack Chambers of the many hats, at one of his famous dinner-parties
Above: Angus and friends cavorting in the newly made goose pond
Below: Tea on the lawn at a children's party given by Sybil and Angus Glendinning. Judith and I are on the left, Stanley on the right

the years, like all rectors' wives, I have had to read in public many times and occasionally to conduct a service. 'It's no bother to you,' people have told me. How wrong they have been. Since that very first time, speaking in public was, and is, a very great 'bother' to me indeed. Two months later Mrs Wynne again paid me a visit to suggest that I should be enrolled as a full Mothers' Union member. The enrolment was held in St John's Church, Laragh, and as Stanley conducted the short service Mrs Wynne accompanied me to the communion rail. As she and I knelt together I wondered how I was going to heave my very pregnant body to my feet again. I needn't have worried; eighty-year-old Mrs Wynne, understanding and kind, put her hand under my elbow and we rose to our feet together.

Our first son was born three weeks later in Stella Maris nursing-home in Dublin. 'We'll call him John,' Stanley said. 'All the churches I have served in have been called that.' My room in the nursing-home overlooked the garden which was filled with sunshine and flowers. 'Could I go out there?' I asked a nurse. 'Oh no,' she replied in horror, 'you might fall.' But I didn't feel at all like falling; I felt very well indeed.

Stanley's parents had been staying with us for six weeks and every day it rained. I couldn't help remembering their first visit to Annamoe and their well-meaning 'pep talks'.

'You may find it lonely here,' my mother-in-law told me, 'But you'll just have to get used to it. It was lonelier for me when we lived in Chile.'

My father-in-law added, 'There's fishing and shooting on your doorstep. Not many people have that.'

Now, on their second visit, Stanley's mother grew more and more depressed by the constant rain. When they left for home she told me, 'In Chile we at least had the sunshine.' My father-in-law was disgruntled too. 'I didn't catch even one damned fish,' he said.

Spring had turned to summer and with it came the flies. We

had never seen anything like them before. During the day they swarmed and buzzed, while in the early morning and the evening it was the turn of the midges. The rectory garden was full of trees, shrubs and bushes and with the river so close it was a perfect breeding place for insects. As summer progressed the horse-flies joined the mob and it was impossible to sit in the garden for long. I covered John's pram, as he slept on the lawn, with a mosquito-net but even so he was sometimes bitten. Judith, too, with her fair skin, suffered. In the surrounding fields the grass was long and lush, the air full of pollen, and Stanley coughed and sneezed. A summer cold, we thought, but when the same thing happened every year we realised that he was suffering from hay fever.

A little distance from the house were the old stables and beyond them was a walled garden, a warm and sheltered place. Once it had been cared for by a gardener but that time had long gone, the flower-beds had disappeared, weeds choked the paths and the box hedges were overgrown. 'I'd like to try and reclaim it,' Stanley said and he dug and manured and planted. That was in the early spring but with the coming of summer the flies descended there in droves, while the midges winged their way from the river. As Stanley worked he was bombarded, bitten and stung. When people heard what he was trying to do, they laughed. 'That garden is a savage place,' they said. Reluctantly he gave up and instead planted new flower-beds on the lawn in front of the house, with a vegetable garden beyond. He still had the midges and the flies but they were a little more bearable there. The bullocks took an interest in the vegetable garden; standing grouped together in the field, they watched him as he worked. Many times the ancient wire fence yielded to the pressure of their huge bodies and they managed to get in. As they thundered around we tried to drive them out. Why was it, I wondered, that this most often happened on a Sunday when Stanley was at church? 'Bullocks,' the children would call excitedly and I would sally forth, on my own, to chase those large animals out. I got quite good at doing it but during our time in Annamoe the bullocks were a constant occupational hazard.

The archdeacon's picnic was held every year in the month of June. This outing for clergy, their wives and families in the diocese of Glendalough, began with a Holy Communion service in St John's Church, Laragh, with the archbishop celebrating. A walk along the shore of the Upper Lake at Glendalough and a visit to the monastic city followed. As everyone settled down by the lakeside and opened picnic lunches a wind would often funnel down from the mountains bringing squalls of rain, and sometimes hail, which sent us all scurrying to our cars. As the years passed the pattern of 'the picnic' changed, for each successive archdeacon had his own ideas on how the day should be run. It became quite sophisticated with lunch in the Royal Hotel in Glendalough and a visit to somewhere of interest in the area. We no longer had to sit shivering on the damp grass by the lake eating our soggy sandwiches. One archdeacon was a widower and shortly before he retired he introduced us to his fianceé, a superb cook. That year afternoon tea was on the agenda for she kindly entertained us in her home. With the appointing of yet *another* archdeacon he and his wife gave us a final outing, a dinner in the Vale View Hotel in Avoca. The 'picnic' had run its course.

The parish year has a form and a pattern to it as season follows season and summer is the time for garden fêtes. As our first fête, which was held at Glendalough, approached it was suggested that I should run a toy stall. In Hector Grey's wholesale store in Dublin we bought some little cars and dolls and that was the beginning of our association with them. Thirty-four years later we were still buying from Hector Grey and I was still running a parish toy stall. A summer visitor to Glendalough, that first year, sent me a box of beautiful hand-made teddies, rabbits and rag dolls. 'Don't sell them cheaply,' she said. 'They're worth quite a lot of money.' But I soon discovered that people were not prepared to pay a realistic price at a fête; everyone looks for a bargain. Those lovely toys appeared on my stall year after year and, although I did sell them, eventually, it was at a greatly reduced price.

As that first fête began, rain threatened and clouds hung low over the monastic city but the stalls did a brisk trade. A large middle-aged woman had donated an evening dress, the bodice heavily beaded. 'Guess the correct number of pearls and win this beautiful gown,' a man shouted, holding the enormous grey chiffon creation aloft on a pole. 'Have you guessed?' the donator of the dress asked me as she swept by. 'It would suit you well.' Two girls sitting on the grass near by giggled together. 'God, what would you do if you won it?' one asked the other. 'Wear it in bed,' her friend replied and they both rolled around in helpless laughter.

Angus had a stall all to himself. He set up a table under the trees and placed a large crate on top with a young goose inside. 'Guess the name and win the goose,' a notice read. 'Think hard,' Angus said to us. 'It's a name you hear often.' But to our disappointment we didn't guess her name – Dilly. 'I did so want the children to have her,' Sybil told me. 'Never mind, we'll give them another goose.'

As the afternoon progressed, the rain which had threatened all day came with a loud clap of thunder. The stalls, which were out in the open, had only a light sacking covering for protection against the weather – I had covered mine with red crepe paper to display our wares. Now the downpour streamed through the sacking covering and ran in rivers over the trestle tops. Hurriedly everyone packed up as the stalls became awash and my crepe-paper decorations turned into a soggy mess, covering my helper and me in bright red dye.

A few days later our goose was due to arrive but tragedy struck. One evening as Sybil called the flock home, the gander, honking loudly in distress, walked alone; a fox had killed his whole family. We didn't seem to have much luck with our pets. In Clontarf our hedgehog ran away, poor old Puss disappeared in Annamoe, and now the goose we were promised had been eaten by a fox.

That August, when John was nine weeks old, Stanley christened him in Derralossary Church. That September, as John slept outside in his pram, Judith and I heard a car coming up the avenue. Parking in front of the house, two men got out and walking to the pram they looked at the sleeping baby. When they approached the front door I got a shock, for both men were wearing purple stocks. Archbishop George Simms and Dr Wilson, the Bishop of Birmingham, had come to visit and Stanley was out. 'It's only a brief call,' they said. And it was, for fifteen minutes later they were leaving. Again they looked at the sleeping baby, one of his tiny hands raised.

'An episcopal blessing perhaps,' Archbishop Simms said with a smile. 'Maybe it's a sign of his future.'

Years later, when John was at secondary school, he was given a list of possible careers which he had to number one to ten in order of preference. He placed The Church last. When asked why, he replied, 'I couldn't stand having to preach all those sermons!'

As the two bishops left, Dr Wilson's eyes ranged over the large garden with the fields and woods beyond. 'It must be lonely for you here,' he said, looking at me with kindness. Stanley was sorry to have missed my visitors for when he was a student at Trinity College, Dr Simms had been Dean of Residence there. During the second world war the Bishop of Birmingham was imprisoned by the Japanese, and like his fellow prisoners suffered greatly but he managed to keep a Christian community alive and regularly celebrated the service of Holy Communion, using rice for bread and water for wine. After the war was over the bishop confirmed, as a Christian, the former captain of that Japanese prison-camp.

For many years it was Dr Wilson who gave the final blessing at the annual Remembrance Day Service in the Albert Hall in London.

Summer was turning to autumn and we had been at Annamoe for one whole year. It was harvest time again with the crops ripe and ready to be cut. We could hear the sound of the combines as they hurried in their work before the weather changed. It was harvest-festival time too with thanksgiving services in our three churches, all beautifully decorated with fruit, vegetables, flowers, stooks of corn and bales of straw and hay. In the country these services have a special meaning for people live close to nature.

Dr Barton, retired Archbishop of Dublin, was coming to our parish to preach and to have a meal with us at the rectory. Entertaining visiting clergy, sometimes their wives too, can be difficult when you have young children. Often it is a mad rush to put them to bed, produce a meal and get yourself ready for the church service. But Dr Barton's visit was one that we looked forward to. Our small round dining-room table, bought at an auction, had a pedestal top which could be tipped flat for easy storing. There was, however, a disadvantage with this arrangement. When in use the top was not too steady, so all our guests were warned, 'Don't lean on the table.' Dr Barton was a great conversationalist and so good were his stories that we forgot to warn him of the table's peculiarities. All went well until, to illustrate some point, he put his two elbows firmly on the table. With a creak and a groan the top began to tilt. Stanley, to counteract the movement, quickly leaned on his side. With Dr Barton quite unaware of what was happening, a see-saw began between the two men. At last the strain grew too much for Stanley. 'Your Grace,' he said severely, 'do *not* put your elbows on the table.' Without so much as a break in his conversation, Dr Barton obediently removed them.

8

Behind the Scenes

During our first winter in Annamoe Stanley had asked Joe, of the village shop, if he knew of someone who would help me in the house. A few days later a woman called at the rectory.

'I hear you're looking for a girl,' she said. 'I've a young one at home who'd work well for you.'

So sixteen-year-old Margaret, with a cheeky tongue, came to help me. We had no vacuum cleaner, only a carpet sweeper and a mop but when I told her this she said, 'A carpet sweeper's grand, I wouldn't know how to use one of them vacuums.' She did work well, with much noise, as she bashed the sweeper round the house and clattered with the mop, dust-pan and brush. I asked her to wash the kitchen floor. 'I love doing that,' she said. Strange noises came from the kitchen, the sound of water swilling and spilling. I looked in to see what was going on to find the floor awash and Margaret, brush in hand, sweeping water out through the back door. It took quite some convincing before she understood that throwing down buckets of water and sweeping it out of the door was *not* the way to wash a floor. She didn't much care for that job afterwards.

Sybil was coming to see me. We had a new china tea-set, bought with wedding-present money, which I would use for the first time. I laid a tray and left it ready in the kitchen. Sybil and I were chatting in the sitting-room when Margaret returned from the village with the day's milk. From the kitchen came a great crash and the sound of breaking china. Minutes later the front door banged and Margaret hurried off home. Sybil couldn't stay for tea and as she strode away in her strong brogue shoes and thick tweed skirt, walking-stick in hand, I raced to the kitchen. The tray was just as I had left it with two plates, saucers and cups, one inside the other but when I picked them up I found that the inside cup, neatly put together again, was completely broken in two. Next day I asked Margaret how this had happened.

'The child done it,' she said angrily, pointing at Judith, 'don't you go blaming *me.*'

The days passed and Margaret spent more and more time in the village collecting the milk. Often she didn't turn up for work at all. She was with us four months when everything came to a head. Outside the rectory front door there was a glass porch, a pleasant place to sit with views across the lawns to the fields beyond. One summer morning I asked Margaret, for some reason or other, to eat her dinner there that day. Stanley carried out a table and a chair for her and placed them amongst the pot plants and the geraniums with the sun shining in. The next day she didn't turn up, or the following one either. Stanley called at her home to be met by a very irate mother. 'My daughter was put to eat in a shed,' she raged. Stanley was mystified but when he realised she was talking about our porch, he tried to explain that we often ate there ourselves. She refused to listen and that was the last we saw of Margaret.

Next there was Bridie who lived with her aunt not far from Annamoe. She walked up to the rectory and knocked at the door. 'I've come for the job,' she said.

'Your missus will have to train her,' the aunt told Stanley. 'She's never worked before.'

Bridie was a big, strong girl and she cleaned as if her life depended on it. 'Am I pleasing you?' she would ask me. 'You're doing really well,' I'd tell her and she'd smile with pleasure. Like Margaret before her, she bashed and banged round the house as she cleaned, especially in the bedrooms until, as time passed, the cleaning noises grew less and there were long silences upstairs.

'Bridie,' I would call, 'what are you doing up there?'

'Dusting,' would come the reply as she appeared at the top of the stairs.

Then one morning I found our bedroom door shut; when I opened it Bridie was busy inside dusting, as usual. In a drawer in my bedside table I kept all the letters that Stanley had written to me before we were married. That day, after she had gone, I found the drawer open and the letters disturbed. I removed them and Bridie must have been disappointed to find her reading material had been taken away. Then articles in the house began to disappear. The cloakroom, off the hall, was large and gloomy, with bars on the windows and wooden pegs for coats round the walls. I kept the pram there and one afternoon as I put it away after our walk, I noticed Bridie's coat hanging on a peg, the pockets overflowing with things belonging to us. Nervously I confronted her and it was hard for me to do it. Throwing the dust-pan and sweeping brush at my feet she cursed me in foul language before storming from the house – and that was the last we saw of her.

The next girl who came to work for me stayed only one day for she was afraid of the long avenue to the house. 'There might be something hiding behind all them trees,' she said.

I was disillusioned and disappointed with our attempts to find someone suitable but when John was four months old a polite quiet-spoken woman approached Stanley in the village. Her daughter was just out of school and would like to work for me. On Kathleen's first morning she cycled up to the rectory on the stroke of ten o'clock, a new apron and a pair of house shoes under her arm. She was a shy, dark-haired, skinny little girl, just fourteen years old. I showed her the house and where everything was kept. She washed and dried dishes, brushed and cleaned, ate her dinner, but not one word did she say. It was at four o'clock, when she was leaving, that she spoke for the first time. In an almost inaudible voice she asked, 'Will I be doing for the children?'

'I like to look after the children myself,' I answered, then seeing her disappointed face, I added, 'but you can help me.' And that, I discovered, was her greatest joy. If John as much as whimpered she ran to him. She helped Judith to dress her dolls and I often saw them playing together. When I took the children for their walk, she would carefully tuck John into his pram and fasten up Judith's coat before running to the garden gate to see if the bullocks were about. On our return there would be a cup of tea waiting for me. She learned to cook a few simple dishes and was proud of her achievements.

But Kathleen's time with us was not without incident. The rectory kitchen was two steep steps down from the hall and every day we carried John's pram down there for me to feed him in the kitchen. Kathleen was clearing the dinner table one day when the phone rang. As I finished my conversation and replaced the receiver, I heard a loud thump, followed by a bang. Hurrying into the hall I found that Kathleen had taken the pram, with John in it, down the steps by herself.

'You should have waited for me,' I told her. 'You could have turned the pram over.'

'The baby didn't mind the bumping,' she answered, 'and I gave him something to play with.'

I looked at nine-month-old John sitting happily in his pram, clutching, in one small hand, the carving-knife.

One November afternoon Kathleen was late going home; dusk had fallen as she cycled off. The next day she didn't appear. She must be ill, we thought, for she was very dependable. Another day passed without her and then Stanley called at her home.

'She's not ill,' Kathleen's mother told him. 'She's had a terrible fright.'

'What happened?' Stanley asked in alarm.

'She saw the pooka,' her mother replied.

'On the rectory avenue?'

'On the road to Tomriland. He came at her out of a tree.'

It took a lot of persuading to get Kathleen to cycle that

road again but she did come back to us on the understanding that she would always be home before dusk. Only once did she speak about what had happened to her and as she talked of the pooka it sounded suspiciously like a barn owl. We did learn, however, that the local people considered that stretch of the road to be haunted and that the pooka, who is an animal spirit, can take many shapes and the sacred month for him is November.

Kathleen was with us for all our time in Annamoe and when we moved to Wicklow she came too, but she only stayed three weeks for she was lonely and homesick without her family. Years later, when she was married and had a family of her own, we met again. Shyly, a middle-aged woman approached me and introduced herself. It was Kathleen. As we talked, the years rolled back and I saw again the young slip of a girl who had been such a friend and a help to us during our time in the mountains.

When we first arrived at Annamoe, Mr Wynne had asked, 'Rayburn working well?' I didn't realise the significance of that remark until later. In winter the house was freezing, except for the kitchen which was the only warm room – until the day the wind changed direction. The chimney for the Rayburn cooker was a tall, metal structure, secured to the roof by two wire stays but when the wind blew from the south-west a down draught was created. We awoke one morning to choking, sulphurous, coke fumes and the kitchen was blue with smoke. This had happened before but that was in summer. Now it was winter and if we put the Rayburn out we would lose our one warm room, hot water and, worst of all, our only means of cooking. We decided to leave it lighting, so that morning we ate our breakfast with the back door open, an inch of snow on the ground outside, while eight-month-old John sat in his high chair bundled up in a large rug. Nothing, we were told, could be done about the down draught so we tried burning turf instead of coke. My

mother said that she could smell turf from us the moment we
entered her house.

We were having trouble with our water supply; it had stopped
again. The first time it happened was on a Sunday when I
turned on a tap and not a drop came out. After Stanley
returned from church he walked up beyond the village to
investigate. Crossing the main road he climbed a stone wall
into a large field where, in an underground cement box, the
water supply flowing from the mountains was housed, to be
distributed, through shores, to the village and to the rectory.
On that occasion a poor frog, caught in the rectory shore,
was causing the trouble. The second time it happened a
dislodged sod of earth had stopped the flow of water, and the
third time, which was in winter, the walls of the underground
shore had collapsed. A major repair job was needed so
Stanley enlisted the help of Hugh, a parishioner, who lived
on the back road from Laragh to Lough Dan. At his remote
cottage he farmed a few acres and kept some sheep but on
Sundays he was at his post in St John's Church, Laragh. The
organ had to be hand pumped and that was Hugh's
responsibility. During the prayers, the readings and the
sermon he sat quietly, waiting, but when it was time to sing,
he leaped into action. It was not a job for the weak but Hugh
was strong and dedicated and could pump vigorously with a
steady rhythm. Occasionally his concentration wandered and
as he faltered, the instrument, groaning, lost pitch. With the
organist throwing him angry glances he would pump his
hardest and the notes would rise again.

On a bitter January day, using picks and spades, Stanley
and Hugh traced the course of the underground water supply
half a mile through the fields to the rectory. The only
satisfactory way to repair it, they decided, was to run a pipe
through the existing shore. Hundreds of yards of black plastic
piping were bought and they began the work. Many times the
pipe stuck and then, digging down through the frozen earth,

they would have to locate the obstruction and free it by hand before they could continue. This hard, cold work took almost a week to complete and during that time there was no water, no heat and no way of cooking in the rectory.

Hugh became a good friend and sometimes he did odd jobs for us at the rectory or helped in the garden. He was tidy and meticulous when he weeded but most of all he enjoyed digging. While he worked he kept a watchful eye on the children as they played outside. Often he would hurry to the kitchen window to call to me urgently, 'Would you come outside please, for I don't like what John is doing.' And I would find that active little boy half way up a ladder or swinging from the branches of a tree.

When the sitting-room chimney needed to be swept, Hugh offered to do the job; he knew a lad who would lend him some brushes, he said. While they prepared the room and moved furniture into the hall, Stanley asked him, 'Have you cleaned many chimneys, Hugh?'

'There's nothing to it,' came the reply.

The windows were opened, the door firmly shut and Hugh began. We could hear the brushes as they made their long journey up through the tall chimney. It took some time but at last the brush head appeared out of the chimney-pot and he had finished the job. Judith was the first to see him when he opened the sitting-room door. 'Hugh's all black,' she said. And so he was, for only the whites of his eyes showed in his soot-encrusted face. ''Tis nothing a drop of water won't shift,' he told us, scrubbing his hands at the kitchen sink. As I walked towards the sitting-room, he called out, 'I wouldn't go in there until the soot settles.' He cycled off, a happy smile on his blackened face for a job well done.

When we did go into the sitting-room we couldn't believe what we saw; the walls, ceiling and floor were all covered with a sooty grime. We spent hours scrubbing and cleaning but in the end Stanley had to repaint the whole room. Hugh, we learned later, had never cleaned a chimney before.

9

Where Does the Wind Come From?

The swallows had gone. One evening we watched them swooping in their hundreds over the fields and the river, to perch for a moment on the telegraph-wires before darting off again. As we listened to their gentle twittering I felt sad for I knew that they would soon leave us. The next day the sky was empty; they had set off in the night for their long journey south to Africa and the sun. My afternoon walks with the children were few now and when we did make it to the road the street lights, up the hill in the village, were often lit. We would hurry back then to pull the curtains, put a match to the fire and wait for Stanley to come home.

Christmas was not far away, our second in Annamoe. As I bathed and fed John one day, nausea swept over me, unbelievable but unmistakable. Morning sickness! Another baby on the way when John was so young – we hadn't expected *that*. My gynaecologist in Dublin confirmed what I already knew; I was pregnant. Later that day I shopped amongst the Christmas crowds in the city and in the evening our friend Jack took us out for dinner. The restaurant was hot and crowded and I felt very ill. On Saturday, as we prepared to return to Annamoe, I got a strong feeling that I shouldn't go. Over the years I have learned to trust my intuition but I was young then, so I said nothing and we left for home. On Sunday the children and I were alone for many hours and it was five o'clock in the afternoon before Stanley was finally home from church. In the evening we listened to 'Letter from America' with Alistair Cooke and to the music of Grand Hotel on the radio while a storm raged outside and rain hammered on the windows.

All that evening I felt uneasy and then it happened. Just before ten o'clock I began to miscarry. I phoned my doctor in Dublin. 'Come at once,' he said. 'I'll meet you at the hospital.' Then I rang my parents to prepare them for the children's arrival. Carefully Stanley lifted the sleeping John from his cot into the moses basket; it was a tight squeeze but he didn't stir. Gently we wakened Judith. As we put warm clothes over her nightie and wrapped her in a rug, she showed no surprise that we were going to visit her grand-parents in the middle of the night. The rain poured down as Stanley put the moses basket and baby into the car. He carried Judith out and placed her on my knee, then battled with the wind as he opened and closed the gates. When we reached the road, the rain eased for a moment, the clouds parted and a few stars appeared. Judith pointed to them excitedly.

'Who made the stars?' she asked, and as we travelled through that dreadful night more questions followed.

'What made the rain?'

'Where does the wind come from?' And Stanley did his best to answer her as he drove through the downpour. In his moses basket John slept on.

But our troubles were not over yet. Approaching Bally-brack, on the outskirts of Dublin, the road ahead was flooded. The car crawled through the lakes of water and the worst happened. With a stutter and a shudder the engine died. It was past midnight and the road was deserted, the large houses on each side in darkness except for one where a light shone. Stanley ran through the rain and banged on the front door. No one answered. Then he heard a car on the road. Back he raced, waving his arms madly. The car stopped and a young man's startled face looked out. Dalkey was only a mile away and that kind young man delivered us there safely. My father handed his car keys to Stanley and, leaving the children with my parents, we were on our way for the *third* time that night. How great the relief to arrive at the hospital, how kind the nurses were. Within minutes I was in the operating-theatre. When I came out of the anaesthetic my doctor was beside me.

'Where's Stanley?' I asked him.

'He'll be with you soon,' he answered.

Stanley was in the lavatory being violently sick.

A few weeks after John's first birthday he stood up and walked and overnight our very good baby turned into a lively, determined little boy. His favourite word was 'no', and he used it all day long. When he wakened after his morning nap he would call loudly 'out' as he tried to unbuckle the straps of the pram. Because he was so adventurous the river was a constant worry. One Sunday morning, when Stanley was away at church, he disappeared. He was there one minute and gone the next. 'Where is he?' I asked Judith in alarm. Hurriedly I searched the many rooms and corners in the large house. I ran outside and looked towards the river.

'He *couldn't* have gone so far, so quickly,' I told myself. 'Or could he?' I shouted his name and in the silence my voice echoed mockingly back. I ran inside again. 'He's *here*,' Judith called. From the sitting-room came a chuckle and, there, in the corner of a large armchair, head down, legs tucked under him, was John, hiding. As he was so active during the day he slept soundly at night. He shared a room with Judith now but he never heard my bedtime stories for he was instantly asleep. If the children slept well at night they wakened early and by six o'clock we would hear their voices as they made their way to our room. Then, snuggled in between us, it was Stanley's turn to tell stories and no one slept through those wonderful tales of faraway places.

Someone had given us two pet rabbits so Stanley made a cosy hutch and a nice big run. Judith called hers Flufty, for he had a soft white coat, and John's grey bunny we christened Humpty. Every day we collected dandelion leaves and watched with pleasure as they daintily ate them and their dinner of carrots and lettuce, carefully washing their faces and behind their long ears when they had finished. Sometimes we brought them into the house where they hopped around and left their visiting-cards on the carpet. We didn't know if they were male or female but when they began to escape we realised that they were both the same sex. First Flufty disappeared and we found him in the vegetable garden, having a feast; he drew blood when we caught him. Then it was Humpty's turn to dig himself out and when he was recaptured Stanley did a major repair job on the wire run. A few weeks passed quietly and then consternation broke out; both rabbits had gone. We searched the garden, looked under rose-bushes, the pampas grass, everywhere, until we saw them out in the field, happily hopping about. Their time in captivity had ended. Some months later we noticed bunnies of an unusual colour in the front meadow; some were fawny-grey while others were brown-and-white. Humpty and Flufty, it seemed, had found wives and raised families.

But if our rabbits had disappeared to have a life of their own, we still had Jumbo and Teddy who were both greatly loved by all of us. Teddy had two white paws, a fluffy black coat, extremely long whiskers and his very round eyes were the colour of amber. He had a wild expression on his face but he was the most gentle of pussies and tolerated being wheeled in the doll's pram and being part of the endless games the children played with him. A window in the basement was always open for him so that he could come and go as he pleased and often, as we sat by the fire on a winter's evening, we would hear a bump below as Teddy returned from his night's wanderings. A loud 'mia-ow' would follow, telling us that he wanted our company. Jumbo's tail would wag as Teddy, with much purring, settled down between his paws to sleep. He accompanied us for walks, dashing from tree to tree and swinging from the branches but he never followed us beyond the outer gate and would be waiting there when we returned. He was a central part of our lives.

One afternoon as we left to visit my parents, Teddy was sitting outside enjoying the winter sun. The children and I were to stay for a few days in Dalkey but Stanley had to return to Annamoe. Back at the rectory Jumbo barked a welcome and Teddy was outside on the kitchen window-sill waiting to be let in. But when Stanley opened the window, instead of bounding in and leaping to the floor, he staggered and nearly fell. Blood dripped from a gaping wound in a paw and one of his beautiful amber eyes, completely out of its socket, hung by a thread on his cheek. With Teddy in a box Stanley drove back to Bray where the vet, Trevor Scott, was waiting for him. As he prepared to operate he carefully examined Teddy. He had been caught in a rabbit-trap, he said, and someone must have knocked his eye out with a kick. It was late when Stanley again crossed Calary bog, the fourth time that day, frost sparkling on the road and sheep looming ghostly white in the car headlights. Next day, in the village, he let it be known what had happened to our little cat but no one, it seemed, knew anything about rabbit-traps.

Teddy stayed with the vet for five days and there was great rejoicing when he came home. The paw healed and the empty eye-socket was clean and healthy. Within a couple of weeks he was climbing trees and going for walks with us again and the loss of the eye didn't seem to bother him at all. Then one morning he didn't get out of his bed.

'Tee-Dee sleep,' John said. But he wasn't asleep. Teddy was dead.

'Delayed shock,' the vet told us. 'It often happens.'

'Tee-Dee gone,' John would say sadly. What could *we* say; how do you tell two small children that their pussy is dead? We grieved for Teddy for a long time and Jumbo searched for him everywhere. We didn't get another cat for we were afraid that the same thing might happen again.

At the south-east side of Annamoe rectory there was a small wood of tall macrocarpa trees growing close to the house. No sunlight penetrated their dark foliage, and the study and the children's bedroom looked out at that sea of gloom and were darkened by it. A path through the trees led to the old stables but I never walked that way for I felt the wood to be a hostile place. On stormy nights, as I put the children to bed, I would pull the curtains quickly, shutting out the swaying branches.

'If we could cut a few of those trees,' I often said to Stanley, 'it would let some sunshine into the house.'

'We'll have to ask the select vestry,' would come the inevitable reply.

Four vestry members arrived and standing at the study window they himmed and hawed as they held a lengthy discussion but at last they agreed that four trees, and no more, could be cut. On a sunny winter's day the first tree came crashing to the ground and its felling was heard across the valley. The second tree followed and in their place was a shaft of sunlight. Three weeks later I miscarried and was in hospital.

It was summer when the third tree was cut but now Stanley was ill with a strange malaria-type virus. As he tossed and turned, with a very high temperature, I was extremely concerned, and not only for him. Rectors' wives have an added worry when their husbands are ill and it is a big one. If a clergyman dies when he is rector of a parish, his wife and his children must leave the rectory within six weeks to make way for the new incumbent. So, not only do you lose your husband but you lose your home too. The only way to cope with that deep anxiety is to put it at the back of your mind and get on with your life. But that worry has a way of surfacing from time to time and with me it was through dreams. The theme was always the same. The children and I were alone and homeless and I was searching, searching, to find *somewhere* for us to live. But the house, when I found it, was always derelict. Walking along dark decaying corridors I looked for one habitable room in which to make a home.

Sometimes the house was half way up a mountain and at other times it was near the sea but the one I dreamed about most was very disturbing indeed. As the children and I crossed its vast hall, statues, crumbled and broken, littered the tiled floor. The room in which we would live was almost pitch dark, its one window high up in the wall and only a curtain for a door. I had that nightmare for years.

The fourth macrocarpa tree was cut a few weeks before Christmas. We had achieved what I wanted; sunlight poured into the rooms. But a week later Teddy was caught in a rabbit-trap. Sometimes, as I stood at the study window looking out at the gap where the trees had been, I wondered about the strange coincidence that after every felling we had suffered a bad misfortune.

One Sunday Stanley returned home from church to tell me, 'We can cut two more trees, the vestry has given permission.'

'We've cut enough,' I answered.

Looking at me in surprise, he said, 'I thought you'd be pleased.'

In front of the rectory, and just inside the garden fence, was a huge oak-tree with great spreading branches. In autumn a carpet of gold lay on the ground beneath as the leaves withered. But the tree had died.

'That should be cut,' people said. 'It could fall.'

'Don't let them cut it,' I told Stanley.

'But this is different,' he said. 'That tree is already dead.'

I watched from the porch as the men arrived and the job began. It didn't take long for the trunk was completely rotten. No misfortune happened to us that time but we never cut another tree.

That year had been a difficult one for us but as it drew to a close I was looking forward to Christmas. I was going to Dublin on the bus, a big event in my life, and had been planning it for weeks. On the sideboard was my piggybank, a happy smile on his china face; I was collecting threepenny bits for my Christmas shopping.

'How are the savings going?' my father would ask me as he put a handful of coins into the piggy.

The evening before my trip I knelt on the hearth-rug and painstakingly removed the money with a knife. It was a slow business. I counted my savings and to my dismay found I hadn't enough for the presents I had to buy. Stanley was reading the newspaper by the fire.

'I need more money,' I told him.

He looked at me over the top of the paper before replying, 'How much?'

'A few pounds,' I answered.

There was silence and when he spoke he was angry. 'Where do you think I'll get that from?'

And so we had a row. I was nearly in tears as I told him, 'If you won't give me the money, I can't go to Dublin.'

'Well *don't* go then,' he answered coldly.

For the first and only time in my life I threw something. Stanley saw the piggybank coming and fended it off. With a crash it landed on the hearth and broke into a dozen pieces. Then I wept, with anger, frustration and sadness. I had come to Annamoe with such high hopes. I hadn't expected the loneliness, the freezing cold or the poverty. Last of all I cried for the poor piggybank, his smiling face smashed beyond recognition.

I *did* go to Dublin. Stanley searched his wallet and his pockets and managed to give me the few pounds I needed.

It was all the money he had.

10

Rectory Life

People are interested in rectory life. What kind of work does a clergyman do? Where is he all day? When his car is outside the rectory is he at his study desk? Is he working at all or just relaxing? What goes on behind the closed doors?

The answer is that rectory life is much the same as in most homes, the highs, the lows and the problems. The difference is in the type of work the clergyman does for he is on duty twenty-four hours a day and is expected, at any hour of the day or night, to put his own problems aside in order to minister to the needs of others. To describe his job is almost impossible for it is so varied with many facets. Teaching, preaching, the care of the elderly and the sick, youth work, the maintenance of church buildings, the taking of services, social work – the list is endless. Everything and anything would describe it better; the whole spectrum of human life is there.

Much is expected of clergy wives. It is taken for granted that they will be involved in all aspects of parish life. Teaching in Sunday school, singing in the choir, playing the organ, running youth groups, addressing meetings, helping at parish fêtes and sales – these are just some of the things they may be asked to do. Not many people think of the fact that a woman becomes a clergy wife because she married an ordained man, *not* because she has a vocation herself. Men and women entering the ministry receive years of training but for wives there is no training at all. Few young women have any idea of what life, married to a clergyman, is going to be like, or the sacrifices they will have to make. It is hard for them to keep their own identity. Even if they work full time outside the home and hold important jobs, in the parish they will always be known as the rector's or the curate's wife and be expected to play a full part in parochial life. Wives who don't work outside the home also find there is a constant tug of war between the requirements of the parish and the needs of their own family. There can be few professions where a wife is so much involved in her husband's work. His demanding job and his long working hours also mean that many clergy wives suffer from loneliness. Often, there is little time left for them to spend together.

For clergy children it can be difficult too. People notice if they don't conform or if they step out of line in any way. Because of this, and especially during their teenage years when they are making new friends and meeting people outside their own locality, rectory children will often not let it be known what their father's profession is. But there was one occasion when John felt it could be a help to him.

The summer he left school he travelled round Europe getting work wherever he could find it. In the south of France he was an ice-cream boy on the beach and when that job finished, and his funds ran low, he had to find work somewhere else. Being a son of the rectory he had what he thought was a good idea; he called at the local priest's house.

'Would you like me to do your garden for you?' he asked. The priest could understand English and his answer was a firm, 'Non.'

As John turned to go he had another idea. 'I could tidy up your graveyard,' he said. The door began to close and John had one last try. 'My *father's* a priest too,' he called.

The door closed with a very loud bang.

Organisations are part of parish life. Youth groups, badminton, table tennis, music and drama socities and many others. It was difficult in our mountain parish to have any of these for the parishioners were widely scattered, the young people few. Every Saturday morning Stanley left the rectory at 9 o'clock for Calary Church, collecting the children of the parish on the way; here he gave them religious instruction but it was a hard task because their ages varied greatly. The Mothers' Union monthly meetings were much valued, for sometimes they were the only social outings for women living in isolated places. Bible study was held every fourth Sunday evening in the rectory and people travelled many miles to attend. One of the members was well versed in the Bible and would have a quotation for every occasion but he really came into his own at the study group. Often, when I went to the kitchen to make tea, I could still hear him quoting chapter and verse in a loud, holy voice.

Stanley attended a course in Dublin to learn projector work and during the winter months he showed films in the hall at Derralossary. In those days when few people, if any, in the parish had a TV those film shows were greatly enjoyed. Before the event we would search the catalogue of films for hire to try and select the right one. Then he would travel to Dublin to collect it and the projector, which was owned by the Missions to Seamen. But those shows could be hazardous, as there was no guarantee that the films, often old, wouldn't break down half way through. As the worn sprockets began to vibrate and shudder, Stanley became adept at doing a quick repair job while the audience waited patiently. Worse still was to find that the ' take-up reel' was missing from the equipment and he would have to improvise one from cardboard and an empty spool of thread. Sometimes this worked well but when it didn't the film on the home-made reel would overflow and snake in a tangled mess across the floor. When that happened the show came to an abrupt end. I could rarely attend, for baby-sitters were hard to find so sometimes, before returning the equipment to Dublin, Stanley gave me a showing all to myself in the rectory.

Sometimes Stanley ran parish socials with games, competitions and Paul Jones dances when everyone was forced on to the floor. But one year he planned a very special event, a dance to be held in Avonmore House owned by Mrs

Ievers. The whole parish was involved in the organising. Dozens of savouries and cakes were baked, mountains of sandwiches made, crates of minerals ordered, cups and saucers were brought from Derralossary hall, and the ballroom was decorated with flowers and greenery. On a beautiful July evening Stanley and I took the road to Laragh and a mile from Annamoe we turned in through the entrance gates and drove down the steep avenue to the house, which was bathed in golden evening light. Mrs Ievers stood on the steps to receive her guests while in the ballroom the accordian, fiddle and drums were warming up. People came early for no one wanted to waste one minute of that special event in the life of our parish. As the girls in their cotton dresses and the dark-suited young men danced, the double front doors stood open to let in the balmy air. Outside couples strolled in the moonlit gardens while the gentle calling of sheep could be heard from the nearby fields. Two hundred people came to that dance from all over County Wicklow and it was talked about for a long time. We had hoped to have another one but a year or so later Mrs Ievers was dead and her house and the estate had been sold.

The rural dean's inspection takes place once a year in all parishes. Appointed by the archbishop, one of his jobs is to see that the churches, schools, parochial halls and rectories in his deanery, which includes five or six parishes, are kept in good repair. On this visit he is accompanied by two glebe wardens and a representative from the diocese, and every third year the diocesan architect also attends. Afterwards recommendations for any work which is considered necessary are made to the diocesan office which then informs the parishes' select vestries. This annual inspection is important but often vestries, for reasons of their own, don't agree with the recommendations and nothing is done. During our five and a half years in Annamoe the only work undertaken on the rectory was the painting of the outside walls. The ill-fitting windows which let the wind whistle through and the tall kitchen chimney with its down draught were never repaired; it was not considered necessary to make the house more habitable or comfortable. Some clergy wives dislike this yearly inspection of their home for they feel it is an invasion of privacy. It is not meant to be, although we did once have a glebe warden who, as he went round, opened our cupboards and wardrobes and looked inside. I *did* resent that.

The telephone plays a large part in rectory life for it rings constantly. Many rectories have answering machines now but in the past these were unknown and as the rector was usually out it fell to his wife to answer it. Children learned at an early age to take messages, writing them down in big childish handwriting which sometimes took detective work to decode and understand. Of all aspects of rectory life I found the phone to be the most disruptive and intrusive. Often, during a family discussion or a crisis of some sort, it has rung insistently at a vital moment, demanding to be answered.

One morning as I was feeding the baby its ringing disturbed us. I answered it. Conversation over and message taken, I continued baby feeding. It rang again; the same procedure followed. The baby didn't seem to mind his breakfast being interrupted but I did. Frustrated and annoyed I took it off the hook and forgot to replace it. A quiet morning followed. Stanley came home.

'What happened here?' he asked as he replaced the receiver. 'I hope no one wanted me urgently.' But of course someone did and had been trying to contact him all morning.

Some people expect *instant* attention when they phone the rector and are annoyed when he is not there. 'Tell him to ring me the *moment* he gets in,' an agressive voice demands. 'Where *is* he all day?' I was once rudely asked. Often as I said politely, 'Can I take a message?' I have *longed* to say something else. But the calls I dreaded most were from people who said, 'I won't keep you a minute,' for those were always the longest conversations of the day. But sometimes, someone *really* needed to talk and if Stanley wasn't there they would speak to me. Then I would willingly listen.

One day an appalling phone call came. As I lifted the receiver a woman's distraught, weeping voice sounded and I could barely make out the words. 'There's been a murder. We need the rector.' I couldn't believe that what she was saying was true. But it was. A fifteen-year-old girl lived with her family in a remote farm-house, reached by a long and lonely path through fields and beside a wood. Every day her mother met her off the school bus to walk home with her, but one afternoon the bus was early. Unknown to her she passed the very spot, amongst the trees, where minutes earlier her daughter had been brutally murdered. It was hard to take in the awfulness of it, the waste of a young life, the shattering grief of her parents and her sister. The parish and the whole community was numbed by it. At the sad, sad funeral, plain-clothes gardai and detectives mingled discreetly with the huge crowd of mourners. It wasn't long before the murderer was found, a mentally disturbed young man from the village near by. The family of that poor girl left the farm and moved away from the area. The land was sold but their home was never lived in again. Today it is a ruin

It was midnight when another distressing call came, this time from the gardai. An elderly man, living alone, had not been seen for some time. He wasn't from our parish but the gardai wanted a clergyman with them when they forced an entry to his home. Inside his cottage they found the unfortunate man who had been dead for over a week. Not from foul play but from a heart attack.

It was also the middle of the night when Stanley was asked a strange question over the phone. A polite voice said, 'Is it all right to use contraceptives?' Startled, Stanley made some reply. 'Thank you,' the man said and rang off!

If the children sometimes got phone messages wrong, it was I who once made the biggest mistake. The clergy in the diocese of Glendalough have a monthly meeting which

begins with a service of Holy Communion. This is followed
by a discussion or a paper being read. One day the secretary
of the Clerical Society, a gentle refined man, phoned and
asked me to give Stanley a message.

'All clergy must attend the next meeting,' he said. 'It's *most*
important that we get this matter settled.'

'What matter is that?' I asked.

'Incest,' he replied.

Stanley looked puzzled when I gave him the message. 'Are
you *sure* he said that?' he asked. '*Quite* sure,' I answered.
When Stanley came home from the meeting he looked at me
with amusement. 'You certainly got that message wrong,' he
said and he placed a copy of the diocesan monthly magazine,
opened at the centre page, on the table. 'What we discussed
was the *insert* of this magazine.'

It was April-fool-day. As Stanley shaved in the barhroom
the children called him urgently. 'The archbishop wants you
on the phone.' Hurrying downstairs Stanley picked up the
receiver and said politely, 'Good morning, Your Grace.' The
children, hiding behind the study door, laughed in delight.
They played this trick with some success at other times too.

In Annamoe we shared a party line on the phone; one ring
for us and two for the others. As we were never sure how
many times it rang we always answered it. One day, as I
picked up the receiver, a woman's voice, low and seductive,
was speaking.

'Is that you?' she said.

'Yes,' came a man's deep husky reply.

'Can you talk?' the woman whispered.

'Briefly,' came the answer.

That call *certainly* wasn't for us, but I listened. The
conversation was hurried, passionate and didn't last long. As
I put down the receiver I was stunned. I knew who the
woman was and the man *wasn't* her husband. Intrigue in
Annamoe! I couldn't believe it. When I told Stanley, *he*
couldn't believe that I had listened. 'You must *never* tell

anyone of this,' he said. I didn't tell anyone but I thought about it a lot! *Who* was the mystery man? I wondered.

Some years later we were at a party in Wicklow town. The room was crowded but over the babble of noise I heard the voice of the 'party-line woman' from Annamoe. Then a man's voice, deep and unforgettable, spoke. Savouring the moment when all would be revealed, I slowly turned round. They were standing, not together, but part of the same group. Amazed, I looked at the man, for I knew him – and I knew his wife too.

Many people call at rectories looking for handouts; some make a profession of it and their stories are all similar. They have come off a boat and need the price of a ticket to Dublin where their mother (sister, brother, father, granny etc) is in hospital, gravely ill. One year the Missions to Seamen, trying to stop this kind of thing, circulated a list to all coastal rectories with descriptions of the people claiming to be seamen. But there were other callers who just wanted a cup of tea. One old man, gentle and polite, came regularly. After he had drunk his tea he would ring the door bell again to say 'thank you'. When he stopped coming we missed him and wondered if he had died. Another man asking for food wasn't so grateful. As I brought him a plate of sandwiches and a pot of tea he looked at them with scorn. 'Is that the best you can do?' he asked insolently. 'What kind of a meal is that for a man? It's meat and spuds I want.'

Then there was the young woman with twelve children who came for 'the price of a cylinder of gas'. But when she arrived a few days before Christmas it was, 'I've come for me Christmas present.' As she left she told me, 'I'll give you *your* present, Missus, in the New Year.'

One early spring evening a man in a dark pin-striped suit, white collar and neat tie stood on the doorstep.

'Are you the vicar?' he asked politely.

'I'm the rector,' Stanley said.

'I beg your pardon,' the man replied, ' I'm English, you see. Could I have a word, please?'

In the study he told his story. He was in Ireland on business he said, and had the misfortune to lose his wallet, credit cards, tickets, the lot.

'This is most embarrassing,' he continued, 'but could I ask you for a loan? I'll send it straight back when my affairs are sorted out.'

I was in the kitchen when Stanley appeared at the door. 'Would you make a pot of tea?' he said. 'Bring it into the study and see what you make of this gent?' As I entered the room the man sprang to his feet. 'So good of you,' he said. 'An embarrassing situation for me.'

He was well-spoken and well dressed but there was something about him that, to me, didn't ring true. As he left with £6 in his pocket (*not* the £40 he had asked for) I watched him from the sitting-room window. As he walked to the gate in his businessman's suit, rolled umbrella in hand, I noticed, for the first time, his shoes; they were white, shiny plastic. Too late, I said, 'He's a fraud.'

We never heard from him again

The American couple, travelling round Europe having a free holiday, were very religious. Their policy was to look up a local clergyman when they arrived in a new town or village, and presenting themselves at his door they asked for lodgings for the night. We were out when they arrived but they waited for us to come home. Spreading out their sleeping-bags and all their gear in the house they made themselves comfortable. They shared our breakfast the next morning and as we ate they preached us a sermon. We are all God's people, they said, and should divide everything we had with each other. They had received wonderful hospitality in clerical homes, they told us, and it hadn't cost them a penny! We found it hard to get rid of them and when they *did* go they left us some cards printed with Bible texts but we received no word of thanks.

The unexpected visit of the two French girls, Anne-Marie and Veronique, was a very different matter. Arriving in Dublin one of them had her passport and travellers cheques stolen. Upset, they prepared to return home but they changed their minds and decided to hitch to the west of Ireland. The priest who gave them a lift was concerned for their safety and invited them to stay in his presbytery for a few days. He advised them that when they visited County Wicklow they should look for some other cleric who would do the same. In Glendalough they were directed to us. They were with us for three days and after they returned to France we kept in touch. They were very involved with Taise, the Worldwide Interdenominational Christian organisation for young people whose headquarters are in France. When Anne-Marie visited Ireland again she and her boyfriend spent a day with us while Veronique, who is now a nun, lives and works in France. They were lovely young women and it was a pleasure to know them.

Redmond was a great actor. We would see him, shoulders back, head up, walking smartly along the rectory avenue. As he approached the house a change would take place; his shoulders would droop and his breathing become laboured. As I answered his ring, he could barely get the words out.

'Is the master at home?' His request was always the same. 'Would you have a few shillin'?'

But one day he asked for something else. 'Would you e'r have an old bed?' he said. As it happened we had an iron bedstead with a horsehair mattress. Redmond was delighted and there wasn't a trace of a wheeze as he asked, 'Could the master run me and the bed home?'

Two days later he was back. 'The bed's grand,' he assured me. 'But would you have the old blankets to go with it?' His wheeze returned, and his shoulders drooped when I told him that I had no spare blankets at all.

But there was one occasion when I gave Redmond quite a shock. It was early autumn when Stanley's mother died in the rectory. A few weeks later Redmond called at the house. He seemed ill at ease and for once didn't ask Stanley for money. At last the purpose of his visit became clear; he had come to sympathise on the death of Mrs Pettigrew. 'She was a lovely lady,' he said. Stanley was puzzled for he didn't think that Redmond had even met his mother. At that moment I appeared at the top of the long flight of stairs, my body silhouetted by the light from the landing windows behind me. As I began to descend, Redmond looked up and his voice faltered and died away. In silence he watched me and when I reached the bottom step, he turned and fled. It was quite some time before we saw him again.

Sometimes rectory families are given presents, a bag of potatoes, a pot of home-made jam, half a dozen eggs. Pattie made the best brown bread in County Wicklow. If we were out when she called, we would find a freshly baked loaf, carefully wrapped, hanging from the handle of the back door when we returned. Olive's barmbrack was outstanding. With a family of ten of her own to feed we wondered how she could find time to bake for us. But one Christmas we received a very unexpected gift. A long, beautifully wrapped box was delivered at the front door. 'Eat that soon,' said the giver. 'These things don't keep.' We unwrapped the parcel and opened the box. Inside was a smoked salmon. 'Happy Christmas to all at the rectory,' said the enclosed card. As we lifted the plastic-packaged fish from its dark green presentation box, another card, not for *us* but for the *giver*, fluttered to the ground; that gift had been recycled! As we slit the covering open, a strong pungent odour hit our nostrils. 'Eat it soon,' we had been told, but we couldn't eat it at all for it was completely rotten.

All clergy and their wives have stories to tell; life in a rectory is never dull. It is also hard work. Most parishioners are friendly, kind and helpful but the rector and his wife need understanding too, for the stresses in their lives are great.

10

Visiting

Visiting his parishioners is part of a clergyman's job, not just the old and the sick but every household in the parish. This is time-consuming and tiring but it is a privilege to be welcomed into people's homes and included in their lives. Occasionally, however, a visit can be an unusual affair. An old man in our parish, a keen beachcomber, lived in an enormous house chock-a-block with flotsam and jetsam which he had collected along the shore. His circumstances were poor and one bitterly cold winter the Eastern Health Board supplied him with vouchers for free coal which he refused to accept, saying he would take charity from no one. Stanley was asked to try and persuade him and called on him one afternoon. The conversation was amicable until the free coal was mentioned. Then the man became violently angry. 'Get out of here, Pettigrew,' he shouted and as Stanley made his way to the door he was given a push for good measure. Some time later the old fellow was hospitalised and when Stanley went to see him he was met with a barrage of abuse from the bed in the far corner as he entered the ward. When he next visited him the man was happily tucking into a tasty tea of sausages, bacon and eggs and it was a shock to receive a phone call the next morning to say that he had died in the night.

Two brothers and their two sisters, all elderly, lived on a remote farm. The brothers had developed a persecution mania and were convinced that someone was trying to take over their land. They spoke of helicopters flying overhead all day taking photographs and landing in their fields at night. One brother took to carrying a shot-gun and once when

Stanley visited them he was met at the gate by a pointed gun, loaded and ready; he was relieved that he wasn't invited into the house. Later, when he heard that the man was taking pot-shots at everything that moved, he decided to give that farm a miss on his parochial round for a while. Some years later the other brother was permanently hospitalised and when anyone visited him he would call out, '*Stay off my land.*' When he wasn't guarding his 'land' he was singing hymns, which he must have learned at national school, for Stanley had never seen him in church.

Ray was a strange, lonely man whose wife had left him, taking their little boy with her. He was not a church-goer, and didn't have much time for any religion at all, but as he was technically a parishioner, Stanley visited him.

One late afternoon the phone rang in the rectory. It was Ray, his voice frightened and on the verge of panic. 'I need you urgently,' he told Stanley. 'Strange things are happening in this house.'

'What kind of things?' Stanley asked.

'*Terrifying,*' came the reply. 'A fire-place has fallen from the wall, chairs are being thrown across the room, and upstairs I hear a child's incessant crying. My housekeeper has left,' he added. 'You'll have to do something.'

As Stanley packed his robes and his communion set, Ray rang again. 'Come *quickly,*' he said.

It was dark when Stanley arrived at Ray's gate. The avenue to the house was long and tree-lined, with branches tossing wildly in a strong wind. Ray was waiting for him at the front door. 'Thank God you've come,' he said. In the drawing-room they sat together while Ray talked. 'It started a couple of weeks ago,' he said. 'First the fire-place fell, then furniture began to move, doors opened and closed by themselves, but the child's crying is the worst of all – I can't stand that.'

'Where do you hear the crying?' Stanley asked.

'In the room that was my son's,' Ray answered.

Upstairs the little boy's bedroom was bright and cheerful,

full of toys, with pictures on the walls. Stanley set up his communion vessels on a small table and began the service. He consecrated the bread and the wine and both he and Ray received. He prayed for peace in that house and for all who had lived or died there. He had almost finished the service of Holy Communion when, without warning, an ice-cold shiver passed up his spine and slowly trickled down again. Although nothing else happened while he was there, he was glad to leave and return home. He never heard from Ray again.

Stanley's parish in the mountains was so scattered that often, taking sandwiches and a flask with him, he was away on his round of parochial visiting for the whole day. The children and I would be on our own until he arrived home again. But sometimes parishioners came to visit me.

Three sisters – kind, middle-aged and all unmarried – lived at Glendalough. Every time I heard their ancient Morris Minor coming up the avenue my heart would sink, for when they called John became very naughty. As my guests politely sipped tea, his attention-seeking behaviour began. He would bounce on the sofa and throw cushions on the floor while the ladies sat tight-lipped and silent with disapproval. A reprimand only made him worse so I tried to ignore him. But when teddy landed on the tea-tray, I had to speak. '*Stop* that, John,' I would say sternly. I longed to banish him from the room but I couldn't; there was no one else in the house to look after him. When the visit ended and my guests prepared to leave they would always say, 'Judith is *such* a good girl.'

But there was one occasion when her behaviour caused disapproval too. We had been invited to their home, a beautiful doll's house of a place overlooking the Lower Lake in Glendalough, for tea. Stanley was coming too and he had given John a stern talk. 'You *must* be good,' he told him. On our way there we collected Judith from school. In the tiny dining-room, when we sat down to tea, I watched John closely but I paid no attention to Judith. I didn't know that she hadn't eaten her packed lunch at school that day and that now she was starving. Sandwiches, hot scones, iced buns, chocolate biscuits, all washed down with rich creamy milk, disappeared inside her, fast. Stanley saw what was happening and tried to restrain her but it was too late. 'I'M GOING TO BE SICK,' she announced. Between us Stanley and I rushed her, gulping and burping, to the front door. *'IT'S COMING,'* she shouted. And it did, all over the spotless doorstep.

Some years after we left Annamoe we met the three sisters again. 'How good the children are now,' they said in amazement. 'It's hard to believe it.'

When I look back at those occasions I remember how formal they were. One in particular I hadn't been looking forward to was the visit of a rather critical, elderly parishioner. But everything seemed perfect on the day she came to tea. The June afternoon was warm, with blue skies and not a midge or a fly in sight. We sat on deck-chairs under the spreading branches of a large fir-tree on the lawn and the garden was looking its best, with roses and lupins in bloom. The sandwiches I made were small and dainty, my coffee cake was light, we drank tea from our best china cups. The children behaved well, the visit had been a success, I thought. *Surely* she couldn't find fault with *anything*.

I was wrong

A few days later Sybil called. 'Your tea-party went well, I hear,' she said. 'But I must ask you, why did you wear evening dress?'

'*Evening* dress,' I said in amazement. 'I didn't.'

'Your guest told me,' Sybil said laughing, 'that you were all dressed for a ball.'

I puzzled over that extraordinary remark for a long time. Could the sun shining on my glazed cotton dress have made it look like satin? I doubted it. In the end I decided that our guest just *had* to find fault with something and that day it was me.

The fact that anyone can call at the rectory leads to some

mysterious visitors. One day a battered old car drove up to the front door and the driver, a small wisp of a man, asked, 'Is the reverend at home?'

'I'm afraid not,' I answered.

'I'll wait then,' the man said. I offered tea and as he drank it he talked of the weather, the crops and the price of lambs. An hour later he looked at his watch. 'I'd better be moving,' he said. ' I've another call to make.'

'Can I give my husband a message?' I asked.

'No message,' he answered. 'I just wanted to see this old house where my grandparents lived.'

'Was your grandfather the rector?' I asked, surprised that he hadn't mentioned it before.

'Indeed he was *not*,' the man said with a laugh. 'We're all good Catholics in our family. He was the gardener here and my grandma was the cook.' Then lowering his voice, he added, 'It was during their time that the tragedy happened.'

'What tragedy was that?' I asked.

'The reverend's poor young wife,' the man replied. 'Just about your age she was too.'

'What happened to her?' I asked uneasily.

'She died,' the man answered. 'Of what I can't tell you but I do know *where* she died.' And he pointed a skinny finger towards the ceiling to our bedroom above. As we walked to the front door he paused and looked up the wide staircase with its gracious curve to the landing. 'These old houses were built practical,' he said. 'There's no way you'd get a coffin down a modern stairs.'

Judith was in bed, recovering from an ear infection, the afternoon the Bartons called. I was reading her a story while John rode his kiddy car round the bedroom when we heard a car approaching, its engine purring. I looked out of the window in time to see a large black Daimler turning the corner of the house. Mr and Mrs Barton of Glendalough House were calling. This would be a formal visit. I had to go down and receive them. The doorbell rang and in the hall

Jumbo barked. As I hurried down the stairs the bell rang again. 'We thought you must be out,' Mrs Barton said as we shook hands. 'Judith's in bed, sick,' I answered, hoping that they wouldn't stay. But they did. They refused tea but as we talked my ears strained for sounds from the bedroom above. Mr Barton, detached and quiet, said little. I longed for them to go but they stayed the required twenty minutes. At the hall door we shook hands again. 'I wish there was something I could do to help you with your sick little girl,' Mrs Barton said.

As their car purred away I took the stairs two at a time and as I opened the bedroom door Judith called out, 'John has eaten those little orange things.' A chair was pulled up to the tall mantelpiece and on the floor beside it, its contents scattered on the carpet, was the bottle of Junior Asprin. From behind a curtain John peeped out.

'How many did he eat?' I asked Judith in horror.

'*Lots*,' she replied.

It had been a full bottle I knew, so with shaking fingers I began to count. Again and again I counted and each time I got a different number. My mind was racing. 'Ring the doctor – eleven miles to Wicklow – and to the nearest hospital.'

To my tremendous relief Stanley came home just then. We counted together. Thankfully, John had eaten only three.

Sybil and Angus were our favourite visitors. We shared a newspaper with them and after they had read it, it was our turn. Every afternoon Angus walked over the bridge and hid the paper in a convenient hole in a tree near the rectory gate. Occasionally we were early going to the tree and the paper wasn't there. 'Colonel's forgotten,' the children would call, and as their young voices carried over the river Angus would come puffing along the road, paper in hand. Sometimes he and Sybil walked to the rectory to deliver it and the children, seeing them coming, would call excitedly, 'Colonel's here.' While he played unruly games with them, Sybil would say, 'Angus dear, you're making the children much too excited.'

But there was one occasion when his visit wasn't appreciated. On a wet cold afternoon, too miserable for our walk, I told the children, 'We'll have a tea-party.' Together we put a small table in front of the fire and their own basket chairs beside it. I poured milk into mugs, made tea for myself and put biscuits on a plate. In the USA assortment there was only one chocolate biscuit and that was the children's favourite, to be carefully divided between them. As I carried the tray into the sitting-room, Angus arrived.

'Anyone at home?' he called, rain dripping from the hood of his duffle-coat. 'Only a brief visit,' he said, handing me the newspaper.

'Have some tea?' I offered.

'Can't stay, Sybil's waiting,' he replied. As he turned to go he saw the plate of biscuits, with the chocolate one, not yet divided, on top. 'Just what I like,' he said, reaching for it. The children watched in disbelief as Angus and the chocolate biscuit disappeared. The disappointment was great, the enormity of it unbelievable, no other biscuits would console them. They couldn't wait for Stanley to come home. 'Colonel ate our chocky biscuit,' Judith told him indignantly. '*Naughty, naughty* Colonel,' John said.

In time they forgave him, but they never forgot.

A painter friend of Stanley's, Carew, often visited us at week-ends. A great nephew of W. L. Wyley, the famous seascape artist, we first met him in St Ives, Cornwall, when we were there on our honeymoon. Walking through the narrow winding streets, we noticed a flight of wooden steps leading upwards to an artist's studio. Climbing them, we found ourselves in a large barn-like room where a group of students were busy at their easels with their teacher, the Cornish painter, Leonard Richmond. Carew was one of those students and it was a coincidence that when we met him again, it was at Glendalough. Gladys Wynne, who was a water-colour artist, lived there, as did Jimmy Esmond, and they, with Stanley and Carew, were instrumental in forming

an art group. They organised an exhibition of their work in a
hall near the Upper Lake and Sean Keating, President of the
Royal Hibernian Academy, opened it. In his speech he said,
'My wife likes Glendalough, but I don't. I can't understand
why *anyone* bothers to paint it.' That didn't go down too well
with the local people.

Driving his fawn MG, Carew would arrive from Dublin
resplendent in tweeds and a long pair of leather driving-
gloves. He wasn't used to children so he always came when
Judith and John were in bed. One evening, as we chatted by
the fire, the wood began to crackle and spark. I left the room
and when I returned, Carew was wearing sun-glasses. Seeing
me looking at him in amazement, he indicated the fire and
said, 'A spark in the eye is a dangerous thing.' And he wore
the sun-glasses for the rest of the evening.

On his next visit, Teddy, who had been lying on the
hearth-rug asleep, stood up, stretched, yawned, and with a
leap landed on the arm of Carew's chair, accidently scratching
his hand. Anxiously, Carew examined the tiny cut.

'Do you need first aid?' I asked, joking.

'Indeed I do,' came the reply, ' for a cat's scratch is a dangerous thing.'

And he wasn't satisfied until it has been disinfected,
antiseptically creamed and plastered.

One summer's evening when he came to dinner the
sitting-room was dark and sunless while the porch was filled
with a soft golden light, the pots of geraniums on the
window-sills were vibrant with colour and the perfume of
honeysuckle wafted through the open door. We decided to
eat there. Carew made no comment on his surroundings until
Stanley asked, 'Isn't it nice here, Carew?' The question was
pondered at length before he replied, ' If you enjoy eating in
a greenhouse, then I suppose it is.'

We were planning a dinner-party. It was Jack's idea for he
liked entertaining. His home, a top flat in Fitzwilliam Street,

was five flights up, the last one extremely steep. Jack Chambers was a collector of antiques and paintings and every inch of wall space was covered with pictures, the rooms filled with antique furniture, silver and glass. An enormous fire was always burning, an opened bottle of claret on the hearth. Jack, who was a bachelor, cooked for his parties himself, slipping in and out of his small galley kitchen while his guests sipped their pre-dinner drinks. At 8.30 pm sharp, the gong sounded and our host would say, with a grin, 'First bell.' Half an hour later the 'second bell ' rang and his guests would take their seats at the long mahogany table in his dining-room. As we ate smoked salmon with brown bread, Jack would invite us to 'Have a little sherry wine.' Succulent rare beef would follow and after that a fruit salad with exotic ingredients. Sometimes, there was a dessert made by one of his lady friends. In his dimly lit dining-room, his collection of pictures looked down from the walls – Nathaniel Hone, Walter Osborne, Humbert Craig, Sarah Purser, and the very valuable collection of eighteenth-century Irish painters, including Thomas Roberts, George Barret, William Ashford and Thomas Sautell Roberts. These he later gave to the Electricity Supply Board for their exhibition room, across the road in Fitzwilliam Street.

Jack's friends were many and varied. Some he had known from his university days in Dublin when he studied for his science degree in Trinity College. Valerie, who was a lecturer in Modern Languages at the University of Pennsylvania, and Kester, the Irish Ambassador in Bonn, with his Canadian wife Elaine, were often there, home on holidays. There were people from the art and business worlds and many others. We knew him as 'Jack', for that was what he was called in his home outside Sligo town, but his city friends always called him, 'John'. There was much laughter, gentle teasing and good company at those parties and as Stanley and I were always the first to leave for the drive home to the country Jack would say with a chuckle, 'The children are going now.'

While we were saying good-bye, his other guests, with much hilarity, would be trying on the collection of hats which hung in his cluttered hall.

Jack liked Annamoe and sometimes he stayed with us for week-ends. 'You must give a dinner-party,' he'd say. 'This old house would look well at Christmas with firelight flickering on silver and cut glass.'

'But we have no silver or cut glass,' we'd tell him.

'I'll lend you some,' he'd answer.

So we planned a dinner-party, not at ice-bound Christmas but in spring when Annamoe looked its best. We invited six people, so we would be a party of eight; but we had a problem, for our dining-room table would only seat four. We phoned Jack. 'Can you bring a table?' we asked. Jack arrived early on the day of the party, a large dining-room table strapped to the roof of his car. It looked well when I had laid it with his cutlery, his silver and his cut glass. In the centre I placed a bowl of fruit flanked by two red candles in tall silver holders, inscribed 'Sligo Club 1812', Jack's christening present to his godson John. We sat down to dinner and firelight flickered on silver and glass. The party was going well and I was relieved and pleased as I made coffee in Jack's magnificent Georgian silver pot. I chatted to our friends as I began to pour, not noticing that the laughter and talk had died away.

'Vera,' Jack spoke beside me, 'I don't think you're handling that pot too well.'

I followed his gaze and saw, to my horror, that a stream of black coffee, overshooting the cups completely, was cascading down the white linen table-cloth in the direction of the guests. The technology of that Georgian coffee-pot had completed defeated me; its long thin spout came from the *side* instead of from the front. Jack never let me forget it. 'And there was Vera,' he would say, 'trying to be the perfect hostess as she poured coffee over everyone.'

12
Weddings and Funerals

A central part of every clergyman's work is conducting christenings, marriages and funerals. In our parish of Derralossary and Calary there were many elderly people so death was a constant reminder of our mortality; christenings and weddings were few.

Every clergyman has 'wedding stories' of amusing or unusual incidents that remain in the mind. I remember the young bride who, emotionally overcome by the occasion, sobbed her way up the aisle and through most of the service; not, I am glad to say, tears of sadness, as she explained in a nice little speech at the reception. Another bride was an hour late. As the minutes passed the tension in the church grew. The ushers hovered at the church door while the bridegroom's father, stony-faced and angry, disappeared outside. But at last the bride came, completely unperturbed, with a rustle of silk and a waft of perfume.

Weddings can be mysterious affairs. On one occasion the appointed time for the ceremony came and passed. The bridegroom, growing restless, walked up and down the aisle. Finally, he disappeared from the church, followed by the best man, his parents and other members of his family. There was no sign of the bride's parents at all and as the few remaining guests also left, we wondered was it a non event? Stanley, waiting patiently in the sanctuary, peered down the now almost empty church while the organist stopped playing to do the same. But all was well, for the bridegroom, his best man and his family returned, to be followed by the bride's parents, the rest of the guests, and, lastly, the radiant bride. We never did learn the reason for that mass exodus.

A couple who came to see Stanley before their wedding listened earnestly as he suggested that it wasn't always a good idea to delay too long before starting a family; they took his advice seriously, for five months later he christened their baby daughter. Then there was the wedding with *three* rings to be blessed. Somewhere between the best man's hands and Stanley's, one of them dived to the floor. It was captured, just in time, as it tottered on the edge of the hot-air grid. Another young couple wanted their marriage ceremony to be 'meaningful'. There were endless meetings and discussions as they tried to rewrite the whole service. The bride had a son, a little boy of five years old, and they wished him to walk up the aisle between them; Stanley wasn't happy with the symbolism of that. The day arrived, and as the bride and groom came up the aisle together the little boy followed, leading all the children from his class in school.

Stanley and I were once guests at an interchurch marriage outside the parish. Heads turned as a world-renowned traditional group arrived and set up their musical instruments on the chancel steps. The air filled with the sound of Irish ballads but few people, in that packed church, noticed the bridal party as they slipped in. The marriage ceremony was brief, over quickly, and then it was back to the music. At the reception the champagne flowed but there was nothing at all to eat.

The taking of photographs can be a nuisance. As the bride arrives a battery of cameras flash and click, while another and yet another photo is taken. Inside the church the bridegroom, more nervous by the minute, waits. When the bride walks up the aisle the photographer bounds ahead. During the taking of vows and the exchanging of rings the camera works overtime, with the photographer peering over the pulpit or hanging from the gallery above, *anything* to get those photos. Stanley once reprimanded an overzealous cameraman; the not-too-polite reply was that he had a job to do and an album to fill. The first wedding that Stanley conducted with a video camera in attendance was quite a performance. Not once, during the entire service, did the bride look at her bridegroom or at Stanley. All her attention was focused on the camera. Later, at the reception, we watched the video and the bride looked beautiful, and very convincing, as she made her vows to the camera.

Diana, daughter of Bobby and Christabel Childers and niece of Erskine, was married in Derralossary Church shortly after we moved to Annamoe. The wedding took place in December and the ancient church, decked with holly, ivy and a Christmas-tree from the Barton estate, glowed with soft candle-light.

But it was the last wedding that Stanley conducted before we left our mountain parish that was the most memorable. Maggie was middle-aged, unmarried, and had a man friend called Tom. We saw them often as they cycled through the village together.

One Sunday, after church, Maggie was waiting at the vestry door. 'I'm getting married,' she told Stanley. 'Me and him will come to see you.'

A few days later Stanley met her man friend. 'I hear Maggie and you are getting marrried,' he said. 'Congratulations.'

"T'aint me,' Tom replied, "tis t'other fellow.'

Maggie and 't'other fellow' arrived at the rectory. 'This is Christopher,' Maggie said. 'He lives over the mountains.' The date was set and the arrangements were made for the wedding. The night before there was a rehearsal but only the bride and groom turned up.

'Where are your bridesmaid and best man?' Stanley asked.

'Them ones can't come,' Maggie replied. 'Them'll come tomorrow.'

The wedding-day was dull and cold but the church glowed with artifical flowers. Stanley stood on the chancel steps as the bride, wearing sunshine yellow and an enormous hat, came up the aisle followed by her bridesmaid dressed in sombre brown. As the service began, the bride, in her large flower-trimmed hat, raised her head and looked at Stanley. With a shock he realised that he had never seen her before. He glanced at the 'bridesmaid' in her quiet brown outfit and Maggie's round, familiar face looked back at him. A quick reshuffle took place and as Maggie and Christopher stood side by side the service began again. The ceremony over, there was the register to sign in the vestry. The bride signed first but the bridegroom, bending low over the long green book, seemed to be having trouble. At the reception Stanley was asked to make a speech. As he wished Maggie and Christopher long life and happiness together the guests seemed ill at ease, shuffling their feet and staring at the floor. There were no other speeches but there were plenty of toasts. With beer glasses raised, the guests called, 'To Maggie and Puddles.'

'Puddles?' Stanley said to the man sitting next to him. 'Is that Christopher's nick-name?'

''Tis his only name,' the man replied. 'I never heered him called anything else.'

On the way home Stanley called at the church. He took out the marriage register and opened it. Maggie's signature was large and clear but Christopher's was almost illegible. Stanley puzzled over it for a long time but at last he made it out. The bridegroom had signed himself Christ!

Country people have great respect for the dead and will travel many miles to attend a funeral. The church is usually packed and after the service, the men, dark-coated and sombre, stand together in groups, the women near by. By the size of a funeral the deceased's worth is often judged. Occasionally the death is of a child and these are tragic and heart-breaking occasions. In our close-knit community it was always a sadness to us and to our Roman Catholic neighbours that, in those days, they were forbidden by their hierarchy to enter a Protestant place of worship. During the funeral of someone they had perhaps known all their lives they were required to stand outside in the graveyard taking no part whatsoever in the service. In interchurch marriages there were difficulties, too, due to the fact that a couple were not allowed to make up their own minds on what religion their children should be brought up in, for this also was dictated by the Roman Catholic Church, causing much heart-break to many families.

Deaths seem to occur more frequently in the winter and the weather for funerals is often appalling. Once, when snow and ice made the roads almost impassable, Stanley had to travel with the undertakers in the cab of the hearse; cars were abandoned by the roadside as the skidding hearse crawled deep into the countryside for the burial. On the day that Stanley buried Gladys Wynne from Glendalough, a gale tore across the land and hurtled round Derralosary Church. Stanley and she had often gone painting together and once, in Glenmacnass valley, as they made their way down to the river they had to climb a barbed-wire fence. Gladys's long tweed skirt was caught on the barbs and, legs and grey woollen stockings torn, she had to be extricated. After that her friends told the eighty-five-year old not to join Stanley on his painting expeditions again. On that wild winter's day of her funeral, with the stunted trees in Derralossary graveyard bending to the ground by the force of the gale, at the very moment of committal, the wind whipped the stole from around Stanley's neck and flung it into the open grave. Was Gladys saying a last, mischievous farewell to him?

It was through tragic circumstances that Carin and her two children came into our lives. Mid morning, on a July day, Stanley received an urgent phone call from the hospital in Wicklow to tell him that a young man on holiday from Sweden had been killed in an accident. At the hospital he met Carin, the man's wife, and their young children, nine-year-old Sara and Thron, a little boy of five. He brought them home to the rectory and we learned the whole tragic story. It was the first trip to Ireland for the family from Overtorneo in Northern Sweden, the weather was good and their week with a horse-drawn caravan in County Wicklow had been a great success. Instead of returning to Dublin for the rest of their holiday, they booked a second week with the caravan company. On that July morning they set off again, Carin and Sara picking wild flowers as they walked along, Christer leading the big, quiet horse down a long gentle slope on the country road, while inside the caravan Thron slept. For some reason the horse broke into a trot. As he gained speed, Christer, reins in hand, ran beside the shafts trying to stop him but he slipped and fell and the wheels of the caravan passed over his body. He died of multiple injuries shortly afterwards in Wicklow hospital.

Carin and the children stayed with us for four days until all the arrangements were made (and the regulations complied with) to fly Christer's body home to Sweden. *Three* times during those four days the poor young wife was asked to identify her husband's body. Her bravery and strength were unbelievable and in that short space of time we grew to love her and her children deeply. The morning we said good-bye at Dublin Airport was distressing for all of us. But they didn't go out of our lives for they came back to Ireland to be with us the very next summer. Hard as this must have been for Carin she felt it was the right thing to do for the children's sake. Over the years they have been to see us many times and when Sara got married she chose Ireland for her honeymoon. We have visited them in Sweden too and seen the beautiful peaceful valley where Christer is buried beside the church where his father was pastor for many years.

It is hard for children to cope with the concept and finality of death. I was six years old when I first became aware of it. As I walked with my father along the Antrim Road in Belfast, two carriages drawn by jet-black horses, black head-plumes bobbing, black harness jingling, passed us and I glimpsed a woman's sad white face at the window.

'Don't stare,' my father told me.

'What is it?' I asked, puzzled. 'Where are they going?'

That time my father didn't tell me but when we saw the black cortège again I repeated my question. 'It's a funeral,' my father replied. 'Someone has died.'

I didn't know what that meant but I guessed, and after that when I saw those carriages and black horses I was afraid. My granny died in Dublin and my father went south for the funeral. All that day I thought about him. Would he travel in a black carriage? I wondered and I imagined his sad white face at the window. Would he cry because his mother was dead? The table was laid for tea, his slippers warming by the fire, when we heard the taxi bringing him home from the station. Joan and Ethne hurried to the front door but I ran upstairs. I heard his voice in the hall as he kissed my mother and my sisters. 'Where's Vera?' he said. As I peeped over the banisters I saw, with tremendous relief, that he was smiling, not crying at all.

One of the most distressing duties a clergyman sometimes has to undertake is to tell the family of the death, often sudden, of a loved one. The gardai too have this unenviable task and it was they who came to our rectory (we were then in Wicklow) with terrible news. My brother-in-law Cecil, Dean of Elphin, had come to Dublin for the Church of Ireland General Synod and he and Joan were staying with us. On a beautiful May evening we walked together by the Broadlough lakes, unaware that their younger son, Peter, had had a terrible accident. Peter was nineteen years old and half way through his degree course in Economic and Political Science at Trinity College. Cycling along a straight stretch of a wide road, well in on his own side, a car approaching from behind, driven carefully and not too fast, swerved for no apparent reason and hit him. He was unconscious when the ambulance arrived and at the Richmond Hospital he was put on a life-support machine.

We were asleep in the rectory, early the following morning,

when I was wakened by the headlights of a car passing over the bedroom window. As the door bell rang, Stanley was out of bed and running down the stairs in seconds. Low voices sounded in the hall and I knew that something terrible had happened. Peter was alive, the garda told us, but he was seriously injured.

Dawn was breaking, the air filled with bird song, as we left for Dublin. In his hospital bed Peter lay so still and quiet, the only sound was from the life-support machine at his side. The doctor came and after consultation with Joan and Cecil, it was decided that the system should be switched off.

As we waited for this to be done something extraordinary happened. The hospital was coming to life for the day. In a corridor a cleaner moved buckets about and as he worked he whistled, most beautifully, *Going Home* from Dvorak's New World Symphony. This was a favourite song of Joan's, and some of the words, which I quote here, comforted her in her great distress, for she knew then that Peter was indeed Going Home.

> *I'm just going home.*
> *It's not far, just close by,*
> *Through an open door.*
> *Nothing lost, all's gain.*
> *Morning star lights the way,*
> *Restless dream all done.*
> *Shadow gone, break of day,*
> *Real life just begun.*
> *There's no break, there's no end,*
> *Just a living on.*
> *Wide awake, with a smile,*
> *Going on and on.*
> *Going home,*
> *I'm just going home.*
> *It's not far, just close by,*
> *Through an open door.*

On the day of Peter's funeral sun poured through the windows of the church and fell in shafts of light on the floor. Wild flowers, picked that morning, mingled with garden blooms. It was a church filled with young people for all his friends had come. As we waited for the service to begin the organist played the beautiful *Nimrod* from Elgar's Enigma Variations. It was not easy for Stanley to take that funeral but it was a service filled with hope in the midst of sorrow. Afterwards, as we had tea in the rectory garden in the sunshine, our two families shared a greater closeness than ever before.

In their tragedy Joan and Cecil behaved with dignity and a deep faith. They felt no bitterness towards the young man who had driven the car that killed Peter. *Why* the accident happened remained a mystery. Back home in Sligo, Peter's sister Heather found some poetry that he had written shortly before he died. In one poem there was the line, ' Why can't we stop the hands of life's clock when we reach the fulfilling stage?' Had Peter reached the fulfilling stage? Did God call him for reasons that were unclear to us? There was something about Peter's death that was hard to explain but which somehow felt 'right'. The day after his funeral I walked alone across the rectory field. Suddenly, I felt Peter's presence, vibrant, full of shining joy and fulfillment and I heard him say, 'Tell them (Mum and Dad) that *everything* I want is here.'

Occasionally, at odd moments in our lives, the 'door' opens just a crack and then we *know* that it is all there, waiting for us, a true beginning and not an end at all.

13

Where the River Flows

During our years at Annamoe the Avonmore River, only three hundred yards from the house, became very much part of our lives. In spring and summer it was gentle and kind. Catkins and primroses grew along its banks and kingfishers darted, their flight so swift they were seen only as a flash of blue before they were gone. On hot summer days when Stanley had cut the large, sloping rectory lawns with a hand-pushed mower, he would run down through the meadow, past the monkey-puzzle to plunge into the cold water and float beneath a canopy of branches and green leaves. But in winter the river became a dark malevolent thing. From the upstairs windows we could see the swollen grey water and hear its roar as it thundered over rocks and boulders carrying large tree branches with it.

At first we only knew that part of the river that flowed through the rectory grounds. But over the years we have traced its wanderings from source to sea. The Avonmore begins deep in the Wicklow mountains above Lough Tay. At Lugalla, the remote Guinness estate, the road winds steeply into the valley below, the encircling mountains rising on all sides. Ruined cottages huddle close to the slopes with small stunted trees growing beside their broken walls. This was part of Stanley's parish and he would drive down the long tree-lined avenue, past Lough Tay, to the low, white, pavilion style house to visit the Guinness family. They were rarely at home, although once when he called a session of traditional Irish music was taking place and he listened as a group of young people played. The steward lived in a large stone house on the estate, with ever-changing views over the valley to the surrounding mountains. In autumn the air was filled with the calling of hundreds of sheep as shepherds and their dogs brought the flocks down from the summer pasture to the safety of the farms below. In the past we could walk our dogs there but it is forbidden now because of the sheep.

From Lough Tay the river travels through a broad valley to Lough Dan. This is the place to see deer crossing the skyline or grazing on the high mountain slopes. In the rutting season the call of the stag echoes clearly on the still air and one day as we sat quietly by the river, a deer, followed by a large antlered stag, ran swiftly past us. The Cloghogue Brook, a small upland stream, gushes down the mountainside, its overhanging banks covered with moss and heather. In the calm deep pools, small brown trout hide between the rocks while grey wagtails perch on stones and black and white dippers bob up and down at the water's edge.

This is raven country and the soft call of 'crock, crock' drifts over the peaks as the glossy black birds soar on the air currents or tumble acrobatically. Here too the peregrine falcon lives and nests on huge cliff faces. Lough Dan is a beautiful lake with sandy beaches, oak-woods and steep rocky ledges along its shore. A herd of white goats roams here, sleeping and dozing in the sunshine or leaping and bounding over the rocks and crags. Once startled they disappear in a moment. At the south end of the lake is a large property, now owned by the Scout Association of Ireland, where young people can camp, canoe, sailboard, climb the mountains and have outdoor holidays. On the opposite shore the lands of Lake Park run down to the water's edge. The poet Richard Murphy lived there for a time when we were in Annamoe and, as his little daughter was the same age as Judith, Stanley took us to visit them once. Driving to that lonely house we could see, through the trees, the lake below us.

From Lough Dan the river flows through tall white grasses, bogland, gorse and silver birches, skirting the Barton estate. One mile north of Annamoe it reappears in a broad green

valley with pine-trees. There is a herony here, their large
untidy nests high up in the branches. Down below in the
shallows the herons, like hunched old men, stand on their
long stilt-like legs fishing or flap lazily over the water. Beyond
the heronry, at the turn of the road, are the remains of an old
mill built by John Hatch, a great-great-grandfather of J.M.
Synge. Laurence Sterne, the author, had a narrow escape
there as a young boy. He and his father were visiting the
rector at Annamoe when Laurence fell into the mill-race and
was carried through the water. Miraculously he came out at
the other end, unharmed. Past the ruins of the old mill the
river flows under the bridge and enters the rectory land.
When Dr Sam Synge was rector there, his brother, John
Millington, was often seen, rod in hand, as he walked along
the banks or even in the river, fishing. As he made his way
home in the silence of an evening, the only sound, it was
said, was the squelching of water from his shoes. Stanley
fished there too but the trout were always small.

From the bridge to the rectory gate is about a hundred
yards and that stretch of river provided us with some
excitement shortly after we arrived in Annamoe. One wet
afternoon Stanley drove down to find a line of lorries and
vans parked all the way to the bridge.

'What's happening here?' he asked someone.

'Filming. We're waiting for the rain to stop.'

A few hours later, when he returned, the rain *had* stopped.
There was great activity everywhere with powerful arc-lamps
lighting up the bridge and the river.

'We'll be filming right through the night,' one of the crew
told him. 'We must get this sequence shot.'

Later, Stanley walked to the bridge to watch but within
half an hour he was back. 'You *must* go and see it,' he told
me. 'It's most exciting.'

Taking Jumbo for company and a torch to light my way, I
set off down the pitch-dark avenue. There was no sign of a
light or sound of activity anywhere; all I could hear was the

roar of the river and the drip, drip of raindrops from the trees. But when I turned the last corner the darkness burst into blinding light as the arc-lamps glared, brilliantly illuminating the old stone bridge and the tumbling river. There were people everywhere but as Jumbo and I moved through the crowd someone shouted, 'Everyone out! We're filming now.' As Jumbo and I hastily retreated we passed a figure slumped in a canvas chair, head sunk on his chest, a rug over his shoulders; Barry Fitzgerald, the star of the film, was fast asleep. Beside him, swimming round and round in a tank, were the fish he was going to catch. Years later we saw the film and the shot of Barry Fitzgerald fishing, which had taken all day and half the night to film, took sixty seconds to show.

The river bounded the rectory land on two sides. Beyond the house were the derelict stables, a favourite nesting-place for swallows. In summer the air was filled with their twittering as they darted in and out of the gaping windows and crumbling doorways, nest building or feeding their young on the rich harvest of midges and flies. The stables were too far away for us to watch their daily activities but one year a pair built in an old shed in the yard close to the house The nest began as a shallow sickle-shaped cup in the apex above the door. It grew slowly as they added straw, hay and grass, all worked together with pellets of mud. It took weeks to finish and we began to think it had been deserted for the swallows seemed to have disappeared. But without our even being aware of it, the female was sitting on the eggs.

One morning, as I looked up at the nest, I heard a tiny sound, so faint that I felt I must have been mistaken. The next day I heard it again, louder, and I knew that there were young ones. Now the parent birds became frantically busy, swooping and diving in and out of the shed all day long as the arduous task of feeding them began. I could see four tiny heads, tightly packed together, peeping over the edge of the nest.

One evening the parents were very agitated, flying excitedly overhead, and we found one of the brood dead on the shed floor. It was a perfect little swallow in every way but much too young to fledge. We wondered, with sadness, what had happened to it. A week later, as I entered the shed, a second sat on the very edge of the nest. Suddenly, with much fluttering, it launched out and hovered, tiny wings beating fast as it looked for somewhere to perch. For a moment I thought that it would light on me but it wheeled and, with a shaky wobbly flight, disappeared out through the shed door. It landed on a bush near by where it sat with its bright beady eyes scanning the sky for its parents, who weren't far away. It wasn't long before it was joined by the other two and as the days passed and their tail feathers grew, their flying improved. Soon it was impossible to tell them from the adult birds. In autumn when they left us we thought with wonder of the long journey of six thousand miles those tiny birds had to make to the warmth and sunshine of South Africa.

A pair of swifts had a nest under the eaves at the front of the house. In our first spring in Annamoe they had raised two clutches there but the following year, arriving late, they found the nest site occupied by starlings. A terrible battle ensued. Hour after hour, day after day, it raged, with the swifts swooping and diving at breakneck speed as they bombarded the nest. Our sympathies were with the starlings and we tried to drive the swifts off with long-handled brushes and mops. In a fury, they dived at us too. At last the battle was over and six pathetic little bodies lay broken on the ground below. The parent birds left and the swifts, triumphant, built their own nest and raised a family there. It was a sad little happening.

Past the stables at Annamoe was the old walled garden and beyond that a large boggy field scattered with clumps of coarse spikey grass where curlew nested in the month of July. We loved to hear their plaintive rolling call and we missed them when they left to winter on the coast. Beyond the curlew field, just before the river left the rectory land, was a large pool, deep enough to swim in. Moorhens lived there and we would see them feeding at the river's edge or skittering for cover across the water as they uttered their loud ' kurrup' alarm call. Sometimes we found them walking with slow jerky steps in the curlew field. If startled by our approach they would fly, low to the ground but surprisingly fast, back to the river. One year they raised three clutches, tiny black spiders that scurried after them or clustered together on the reeds. Moorhens are fiercely territorial and when a mallard and her family entered their pond, the parent moorhens drowned the tiny fluffy ducklings one by one, while the poor mother duck, unable to protect them on her own, watched helplessly and in great distress.

It was here that we sometimes saw signs of an otter, the marks of his webbed feet showing clearly in the mud. Shy and wandering, it is extremely difficult to catch a glimpse of these beautiful creatures. One calm early morning with the light dancing on the water, as Stanley walked across a bridge over a tidal estuary a movement in the river underneath caught his eye. Leaning over the parapet he saw the water below swirling in circles. Expecting a diving cormorant to surface, he was surprised when a large flat head appeared. To his amazement it was an otter, long whiskers showing plainly in a dark face, an eel held firmly in his mouth. Quite unperturbed by Stanley's presence he swam under the bridge, his long thick tapering tail stretched out, rudder-like, behind him. Climbing on to the shore, his sleek damp body glistening, he proceeded to eat the still wriggling eel. When Stanley left, the otter was still enjoying his breakfast.

Where the river leaves the rectory land it enters the Avonmore estate. It is along stretches such as this that mink can be found. Originally farmed for their skins they have escaped all over Ireland and have become established in the wild. In appearance they are like small otters but while otters are shy and retiring mink are fearless and vicious killers. Twice I have had encounters with them. On the first occasion one slid through a small gap at the bottom of the wire netting of my duck-run and grabbing my duck Diana by the legs he dragged her to the hole; luckily she was too large to fit through. Hearing the commotion I hurried out but the mink, not in the least afraid, continued to try to pull her out. It took a lot of banging on the wire and shouting by me before he released her. Thankfully she survived the shock and lived to a good old age. Not so lucky was the duck who decided to take a walk *outside* her run. Scrambling through a thick gorse and bramble hedge she gained access to the outside world. I found her, badly mauled and dead, close by. I thought it was the work of a fox but a few days later panic again erupted in the duck-run. This time the mink was *inside* the fence and was chasing the unfortunate drake. I could see the creature's evil face as he surged through the water. Only after much arm waving and stone throwing did he leave. The duck-run was repaired and the ten-year-old drake lived on.

After passing through the Avonmore estate the river flows between deep woods and farmland past Trooperstown hill to south of the village of Laragh. Here it is joined at Bookeys bridge by the Glenmacnass River where it becomes broad and wide and the valley is deep. The little church at Clara stands at the water's edge, the hills rising steeply on either side. Under the arched humpback bridge the river flows on through oak-woods, then skirting the village of Rathdrum it travels under the bridge beside the old flour-mill, to meander in a wide arc until it enters Avondale estate, the birth-place of the Irish patriot, Charles Stewart Parnell. One of eleven children, he had a privileged childhood, growing up in the beautiful parkland surrounding his home. The 530 acres of land is now a school of forestry, with broad rides between the trees, many of which are two hundred years old. There are river walks and house and grounds are open to the public.

Some miles beyond Avondale, at the meeting of the waters at Avoca, the Avonmore is joined by the Avonbeg and together they flow through the beautiful but mine-scarred Vale of Avoca to Arklow. North of the harbour, where the river flows beside the main street, dozens of swans can be seen.

In a quiet river tributary I once witnessed the mating ritual of two swans. With long slender necks held high, then arching downwards, they dipped their heads deep in the water. Over and over, in perfect harmony, they performed this graceful movement. Then the male stretched his neck over the female's and they remained, necks entwined, for a few moments. The final coming together was swift, over in seconds, but very gentle. Afterwards they bathed, preened and disappeared side by side upstream. Swans mate for life and this couple had been together for a long time. Their enormous nest was built in the reed beds and we often saw the pen's long neck raised, looking around her, as she sat on the eggs. The cob was a very fine bird who patrolled his territory and guarded her fiercely; it was never safe to go too close. Once we saw him chase two terrified canoeists until they abandoned their craft on the shore and ran. Year after year the swans raised a family of three or sometimes four. We would see them sailing along on the river, one parent in front, the other behind, the grey cygnets in between.

One spring a very high tide washed the swan's nest away and we thought there would be no young that year but they must have built again in a safer place, for as spring turned to summer they appeared with three large cygnets. In late winter the parent birds drive away the offspring they have cared for so devotedly and they are left to their own devices. It is sad to see this rejection but the cygnets, now full grown, soon join a band of other young swans.

At Arklow, once an important seaport, where the first lifeboat station in Ireland was opened in 1824, the Avonmore has one more bridge to pass under before it flows through the harbour. With gulls wheeling and screaming overhead, its long journey from the Wicklow mountains over, it enters the sea.

14

A Country Christmas

Dan was ploughing; the November mist rose from the valley as gulls wheeled over the tree-tops. It was always a mystery where they came from for, at Annamoe, we were eleven miles from the sea. We loved to watch Dan working; no noisy tractor belching fumes turned the furrow as he ploughed with a horse. Quietly, with the steady rhythm of man and horse in harmony, the large gentle animal moved over the brown earth, his great feathered legs spattered with mud. In the still air the only sound was the jingle of harness and the occasional snort from the horse. A little breeze arose and his black mane stirred and his tail flowed. Behind the plough, rising and falling backwards and forwards, the gulls flew.

Dan's field on the back road to Moneystown was near the entrance gates to Castlekevin. Half a mile further on was the Beltons' farm-house with flagged floors, oil lamps and crickets on the hearth. Many times Stanley returned home from visiting this kind elderly couple to tell us that as they sat by the large open fire-place the crickets had appeared to sing loud and long. One afternoon the children and I went there with him. It was dusk when we arrived for crickets are nocturnal and we didn't want to be too early for the concert. The kitchen was shadowy, lit by an oil lamp on the dresser and a glowing wood fire. We sat and waited. And waited. But there wasn't a sign of the crickets. 'The wee men are shy tonight,' Willie said. Disappointed, it was time for us to leave. Outside it was very dark but as Willie guided us to the car with a lamp Kathleen called softly from the house, 'They've come.' We tiptoed back and sitting on the hearth, singing their hearts out, were two large fat crickets.

It had been raining for a week. Not just a shower but a steady downpour. We were confined to the house and with no TV or video films to pass the time, and no car to take them for a drive, the children were bored and frustrated. The toys they had were simple, the most prized being a box of clothes for dressing up. Old clothes, curtains, scarves, hats, anything with a bit of glitter, gave them hours of fun; 'make believe' was high on the agenda. But after several days of rain something new was needed. I planned a wedding. John's Teddy was to marry Judith's doll. The big day arrived and the cake, encrusted with white icing, stood on a table in the playroom. To the strains of *Land of Hope and Glory* on the gramophone Judith prepared to carry the bride up the aisle. Then she caught sight of the wedding-cake with a bite taken from its side. Investigating further, we found that John had eaten a large piece. Banished from the proceedings, he spent the afternoon happily with Stanley, for he had grown bored with the whole event. By bedtime he wanted Teddy back, so for Judith's doll married life was short. The wedding hadn't been a great success but the preparations for it had helped to pass a few wet days and at last the rain had stopped and our daily walks could continue.

If entertainment for the children was scarce, for me, apart from the formal tea-parties and the occasional caller, it was practically non-existent. Those were the days of dress dances and in Annamoe I often looked at my evening gowns, most of them made by my mother, hanging in the wardrobe and I wondered if I would ever wear them again. Shortly after we came to the rectory we were invited to the County Wicklow Scout Association dance in Bray. I was excited as I washed my hair and ironed my dress in preparation for the event but as the day wore on Judith became ill and ran a high temperature; the doctor told us that she had an ear infection. As I put away my dress, sequinned handbag and high-heeled shoes, Stanley said, 'Don't be disappointed. We'll go to a dress dance some other time.' But it would be seven years before we went to one again and that was after we had left Annamoe.

One of the dresses hanging in my wardrobe was a pale-blue slipper satin, its high neckline embroidered with a silver butterfly, the shoulders swathed in soft folds of material. The first time I wore it was when I was still at school. My aunt and uncle, Jessie and Reggie Brownell, gave a dance for their two university-student daughters and it was held in Belfast Castle, a romantic place with turrets and terraced gardens overlooking Belfast Lough. Those were the days of bouffant-skirted evening dresses with low bodices. There was no such creation for me but on the night of the dance when I put on my blue dress and it fell in a shimmering cascade to my feet both my mother and I were pleased with the result. But at the dance I felt young and unsophisticated, for all the other girls were glamorous in their décolleté strapless tops and swirling skirts I hadn't been asked to dance much when the MC announced, 'Find your supper partner by matching the numbers on your cloakroom tickets.' I found my partner all right but he took one look at me and disappeared. The embarrassment of it was awful. Would I have to eat alone? But my sister Ethne and her partner took pity on me and I joined them for supper.

I wore my blue satin dress again at Stanley's degree-conferring dance in the Metropole ballroom in Dublin, but I had a problem with it. The folds of material covering my shoulders were draped so tightly that I had trouble raising my arms when I danced. With elbows clamped to my sides I just about managed it, but if I raised them too high I felt the material began to tear. The evening drew to a close and Stanley still hadn't admired my dress. I *had* to know what he thought of it. 'Do you like it?' I asked him. There was a pause before he replied, 'It's nice but you're very covered up!'

He must have thought the same thing the previous night when he took me to a film. As I got ready in the bank house in Phibsborough, where I was staying with my aunt and

Michael, who was born just
before we left Annamoe
(*Photo Kay Mullen*)

Michael's christening.
Judith's German dress was a gift
from the Baders

Not strictly from our Annamoe days but it sums up all those
summers of sea and sand

uncle, Dorrie and Joe Armstrong, I was in a dilemma. I had a
new winter coat but before I left Belfast for Dublin my
mother said, '*Don't* get your new coat wet.' I also had a thick
rubberised riding-mac with me and in Dublin it was drizzling
rain. Which should I wear? After much thought I decided to
wear *both* of them. As we arrived at the Theatre Royal the
stage show with the high-kicking Royalettes was ending. To
the strains of the Warsaw Concerto we were shown to our
seats. In the darkened cinema Stanley helped me off with my
mac but as he sat down he noticed that I was struggling to
remove a second coat of thick tweed with a wide leather belt.
With a look of surprise on his face he helped to divest me of
that one too. 'You wear a *lot* of clothes,' he said as the film
began.

Usually Judith and John played well together which was
lucky for there were no other children nearby. Judith's
favourite game was 'air hostess' (the result of taking them to
Dublin airport to see the planes landing and taking off), so
Stanley made a cardboard plane which covered the entire
floor space of the empty dining-room. Inside, the teddies and
dolls sat in rows while Judith, dressed in green, moved up and
down the aisle serving food. John wanted to play. 'You can be
the engine,' she told him. So John sat in his chair at the front
of the plane and made engine noises. 'I'm tired, Judy,' he said
after a while. 'This plane won't fly without an engine,' she
told him sternly. So the poor engine 'wa-a-a-n-ed' on and
on. But John was a man of action and he had had enough.
With cries of dismay from the air hostess, he flung the
passengers to the ground and turned their seats over. After
that the plane flew engineless.

Harry, a friend from our Clontarf days, was John's
godfather. He was popular with the children and when he
stayed with us the fun began in the early morning when they
knocked on his door, calling, 'Breakfast ready, Harry.' Not a
sound from inside the room. After a second and sometimes a
third knock, they would open the door a crack and peep in,

to find bed and the room quite empty. 'He's *gone*,' John would say anxiously. At that moment Harry would leap from his hiding-place behind the door and there would be shrieks of laughter through the old house.

But there was one occasion when Harry's fun didn't go as planned. A few weeks before Christmas we took the children to Bray to see Santa. We drove through Roundwood, passing the shop where the Christmas decorations stayed up all year, over Calary bog and down the Long Hill to Kilmacanogue. At Bray a disappointment awaited us, there was no Santa in the town at all. But unknown to us a Father Christmas was on his way to Annamoe along the very route we had just travelled. At the rectory gate he parked his car and took out his gear – tall black boots, red coat and hat and a long white beard. Shouldering his sack he walked up the avenue. Near the monkey-puzzle he turned right and, struggling up the steep hill to the meadow in front of the house, he lifted his sack over the garden fence and climbed after it. Not a sound disturbed the stillness. No children played in the garden or looked out of the windows. 'There must be *someone* here,' he thought.

There was; at the back of the house standing by the clothes-line, pegs in hand, mouth wide open in shock, was Kathleen.

'Where's everyone?' he asked.

'Bray,' she replied in a whisper.

As he left, Santa looked back. Kathleen, pegs still in hand, mouth still open, was rooted to the spot watching him.

When we arrived home she met us at the front door. 'Santa was here,' she said. 'He left presents.'

Later that day I asked her, 'What did you think of him?' She gave the question deep thought before she replied, 'He was nice.' And that was the end of that!

Derralossary Church, two miles from the rectory, was where we took the children each Sunday. The old horse-box pews were a perfect place for John to look at his picture books and play with dinkie cars without being seen. But sometimes the tiny cars became noisy; then Joe, of the

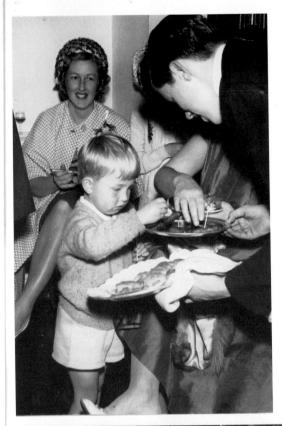

Left: Member of the wedding – John makes a serious choice; I'm in the background (*Photo Rex Roberts Studios*)
Below: All but one of my family – parents Tom and Eva, sister Ethne and her son Timothy

Tea at the Baders. I'm in the background with their baby Christine.
In front: Lore, John, Margaret Bader, Judith and Stanley

Farewell to Annamoe: J. B. Wynne makes a presentation to us.
Parishioner Willy Belton can be seen in the background

Left: Stanley at his easel, attired for all-weather painting
Below: Me, in our new home in Wicklow, with Lir, our bearded collie. (*Photo Passerose Mantoy*)

grocery shop in Annamoe, would look round at us sternly. One Sunday John grew bored and as he fiddled with the catch on the door of the pew, it opened and he stepped into the aisle.

'I'm going to run up to Daddy,' he told me.

'No,' I whispered. 'You musn't.'

John smiled sweetly and taking up a running position, his voice rising with every word, he said, 'I *will* run up to Daddy, I **will**, I WILL.'

The whole congregation of ten elderly people turned round and looked at us. From his reading-desk Stanley summed the situation up and knowing that John's exuberant behaviour would not be tolerated, or understood, by those conventional old men and women, he mouthed at me, 'Out!' And out we went, John protesting loudly while Judith, head down in embarrassment, followed. Outside the sun shone, the birds sang and John recovered quickly from his eviction but Judith was upset by the indignity of it all. After that, every time we met Joe he would look at John disapprovingly and say, 'Are you being a good boy, now?'

The annual carol service at Derralossary was held on the Sunday evening before Christmas. The church was very cold – the few small oil-heaters did nothing to dispel the damp – so I dressed the children for the occasion as if they were going to the North Pole. As I piled layer upon layer of clothes on, John would call excitedly to Harry, who was staying with us, 'Ready, Harry?' As we drove to the service our breath smoked in the cold, unheated car. The old church was decorated with holly and a Christmas tree at the chancel steps, its 120 candles, their brass holders entwined with ivy, flickering violently in the draughty air. Members of Rathfarnham parish in Dublin, which was linked with our parish, had come with their choir. As the harmonium creaked and groaned into life and the church filled with the singing of ancient carols, John sang too. He sang during the verses and between the verses.

A little girl seated at the front of the church asked her mother, 'Why is John crying?'

'He isn't,' her mother told her, ' he's enjoying singing.'

Over the years a little ritual developed in our home on Christmas Eve. Just before bedtime, and the traditional leaving of a glass of milk and mince-pies on the hall table for Santa Claus, we would have our *own* carol service. Kneeling beside the Christmas-tree in the sitting-room, its branches shining with lights, decorations and tinsel, we would sing our favourite carols. But the one who sang best, his eyes raised to the golden star at the top of the tree, was always John.

Twice that Christmas the children had been disappointed to miss Santa, so we took them to Dublin to see the lights. The streets were crowded as we battled our way past the brightly lit shop windows and into the toy department of a large store. They looked in wonder as automatic toys clicked and whirled, toy trains sped past and dolls in beautiful dresses smiled from their boxes. 'Would you like a truck?' Stanley asked John, pointing to a large display, 'or a gun, or a boat?' John, his face scarlet with excitement, hurried from toy to toy but he just couldn't decide. It was all too confusing. Judith also was having problems as to what to buy, for the budget was small. After much changing of minds and arguing, with tears not far away, they made their choices. A long queue had formed for Santa and his expensive gifts. 'He's not the real one,' we told the children. 'The *real* one will come to you on Christmas Eve.'

Outside in the street the Christmas lights were switched on as we battled our way through the crowds. One of the highlights of that trip was to be tea in a café in town, a treat the children had never had before. The Country Shop on St Stephen's Green was informal and welcoming, the perfect place to take the children, we thought. In the basement café a smiling, grey-haired lady escorted us across the red-tiled floor. The plain wooden tables were covered by bright checked cloths, a dresser along one wall was filled with pots of jam, marmalade and home-made cakes. We ordered tea but both children were strangely silent. We asked them what was wrong but neither would tell us.

However when they next saw my parents they told them, 'We had tea in a *kitchen*, it wasn't a café at all.' But that evening, as we drove home, Stanley and I had something else to worry about; it had started to snow.

The first flakes fluttered down near Bray. By the time we reached Kilmacanogue and turned up the Long Hill, it was falling fast. The last three hundred yards to the plateau are very steep and to our dismay the car slithered to a halt. Many times Stanley tried to get a grip on the snow but the wheels just spun round. 'You'll have to get out,' he told us. 'I might make it to the top of the hill if the weight is less.' As we climbed from the car the children were very quiet. Stanley placed mats behind the rear wheels and I got ready to push. It worked. The car crawled up the hill and, to the children's consternation, disappeared from sight. But soon Stanley was back for us, his feet slipping and sliding on the icy road. The relief was great to find the car just over the brow of the hill. The journey home took a long time as the snow on Calary bog was deep. We met no other traffic, we were quite alone in a white wasteland. As we crawled along, the wipers did little to clean the driving snow from the windscreen. Annamoe's three lights never looked so welcoming as they did that evening when we arrived home.

'We won't tell my parents about this adventure,' I said to Stanley. 'It would upset them.' But we had reckoned without John, for he told them the whole story. 'Mummy pushed and pushed in the snow,' he said, 'and the car zoomed up the hill.' My parents *were* upset and not impressed, as John was, by my show of strength.

15

A Painter's Life

Thursday was Stanley's day off, unless someone wanted him for something – and they often did. But if there were no emergencies or last-minute calls, he was free to pursue his lifelong interest. He was first introduced to painting when he was a boy in Sligo by Jim Houston who lived in a cottage almost at the water's edge at Gibraltar, a wide expanse of mud flats when the tide went out, three miles from Sligo. Stanley and his friends had made a black tarred canoe, which they called the coffin, and bringing it down to Gibraltar on a cart pulled by a donkey they launched it. From the nearby cottage a man watched them with interest. When the three very wet boys had had enough canoeing the man invited them to leave their craft in his back yard. 'Now I'll show you what *I* do,' he said and inside his cottage the boys admired his many colourful paintings. Soon Stanley and Jim would go on expeditions together, cycling all over County Sligo. Once they were joined by a Frenchman who liked to paint looking backwards between his legs! As they walked over the sands at Culleenamore, the day after the flapper race-meeting, the Frenchman gleefully picked up a tide-washed pound note which later Jim made him spend in Mikey Brees' pub in Strandhill.

By profession Jim was a sign-painter. In his youth, in 1916, he had spent time in prison for his activities in the IRA, and six years later, after being captured in Ballymote Church tower, he was again imprisoned. He was an interesting character and I enjoyed visiting him and his wife Isobel; the kettle would be on the stove even before Stanley and I reached the front door. After the two men had discussed painting and we were about to leave, Jim would hurry to the sideboard and take out a bottle of home-made wine. Then a second bottle would be placed on the table.

'Not *that*, Jim,' gentle Mrs Houston would say in alarm.

'This is for *me*,' he would reply, and pouring out a good measure of poteen he would sip it with satisfaction.

When Stanley was a student in Dublin he made the aquaintance of Tom Nisbet, Ireland's leading water-colour artist, who had a gallery off Grafton Street. One day Stanley went there to look at the paintings and from his underground workshop, where he made frames, the artist appeared. And that was the beginning of their friendship. Often Stanley, weary with studying, would leave the reading-room in Trinity College and walk up to the Grafton Gallery to chat with Tom. As he made frames he patiently listened to Stanley's worries about history and political science which he was studying at the time. Once he met Brendan Behan, whose portrait in oils Tom was painting. When Stanley returned from his holidays in Sligo he would show Tom, who was well known for his sincere but sometimes shattering criticism, his paintings. However it was because of this that Stanley made progress. Eventually Tom encouraged him to submit pictures to the Royal Hibernian Academy's annual exhibition in Dublin. When, after many disappointments, he was accepted, his joy was great.

Since that first time Stanley's light-filled paintings have been hung many times in the RHA's annual exhibition. As one queues with the other invited guests on the opening night to meet the President of the Academy, a small orchestra plays. Upstairs the airy Gallagher Gallery is thronged and it is often difficult to see the paintings. It is always a thrill to find the coveted red spot on Stanley's picture which means it has been sold. Each year he has his own exhibition in either Dublin or locally in Wicklow and then too the red spots on the pictures are exciting, representing the reward for many months of hard painstaking work.

The basement at Annamoe did have one advantage; Stanley could keep his easel, paints, palette, turpentine and brushes, all the paraphernalia of the artist, in a room there but all his painting was done out of doors. He has always been haunted by reflections. Childhood memories have remained with him of sailing home from one of the islands on Lough Gill. As the boat glided across a mirror of reflections of quivering reeds and the dark green foliage of the wooded islands, there were ripples of gold and silver from the evening sky. Reflections on water and huge sky-scapes are his favourite themes. Sligo was his original inspiration; now most of the year he paints in County Wicklow.

But of all places in Ireland it is Connemara, the most westerly part of County Galway, that he loves to paint. The stark rugged landscape with its many stone walls is extremely beautiful but it is also a very wet part of Ireland. The Atlantic winds carry sheets of rain over the bogland and lakes, while mists often blot out the grandure of the mountains. But when the sun shines, the landscape dazzles, with scintillating colour lighting up the dark lakes and tumbling rivers, and casting long shadows over the sweep of the Twelve Bens. With its many curragh-filled harbours, with perhaps a Galway hooker swinging on the tide, miles of fine white sand, great stretches of bogland, it is unendingly fascinating for a painter.

We have holidayed in Connemara since the children were small, in a caravan on the O'Malley land overlooking the tidal island of Inis Doras near Ballyconnelly. Every day, when the tide was out, we would watch Rita driving her cows over the wide strand to the island where they would graze. Then, when the tide went out again, they would make the return journey to the mainland. One cow we nicknamed the 'submarine cow' because, anxious to get home, she often left the island when the water was still deep; we would see her swimming strongly for the shore, with only her head showing above the water.

Mason Island is two miles off the coast of Connemara. The original inhabitants were fishermen and boat builders but since the last family moved to the mainland in 1950, the island has been deserted. My sister Ethne owns a cottage there beside a tiny tidal cove with the Aran Islands in the distance. At low tide the cove is alive with feeding birds and the piping of oyster-catchers fills the air. Close by is the tidal Oilean Aill na Croise, where nesting roseate terns, with high-pitched angry cries, dive-bomb anyone who goes too close. The island road, now covered with short grass and moss, winds between stone walls from the harbour to Trá Bán. Another road going from east to west meets it at the highest point of the island where the views across the water to McDara's Island with its high Celtic church and the Twelve Bens are dramatic. It is a peaceful place, cut off from the outside world, only accessible by boat across a two-mile stretch of water. The first few times we went there for holidays we were ferried across the water by eighty-four-year-old Joe Casey, who was born and brought up on the island. Pipe in mouth he would skilfully negotiate the often choppy crossing and the tricky narrow rockstrewn entrance to the harbour, in his one-hundred-year-old boat.

Stanley has painted many pictures of Mason Island, sometimes in wind and rain, when he would return to the cottage soaked to the skin. Hanging his wet clothes to dry on a line strung across the living-room, the cast-iron stove would be stoked with driftwood collected from the shore to make a good fire. As we looked at his new picture Stanley would stride around the room to find the right place to display it in the best possible light.

'Don't touch it,' he would say if someone came too close. 'It's wet, you know.'

'He's ruthless where his paintings are concerned,' I'd tell Ethne and her family who would laugh and say, 'Stanley ruthless? Never.' But one day they witnessed that side of his nature. We were leaving the island, our holiday over, and as we walked to the harbour for the boat, Stanley carefully carried one of his pictures. I am not a good sailor and that two-mile crossing to the mainland is often rough. I was apprehensive as our gear was stowed and I waited for Stanley to help me into the swaying craft. But to my surprise he quickly stepped past me and sat down in the most sheltered spot, cradling his picture in his arms. Fortunately my nephew Tim was there to give me a hand. We set off into the wind and the rain, Ethne, her family and another couple waving good-bye. When we were well out of earshot, or so I thought, I gave Stanley a piece of my mind for being so ill-mannered and callous to me. But every word I said and his reply, 'I *must* protect my painting,' was carried back to the farewell party on the harbour wall, much to their amusement. We arrived wet and bedraggled and had to retire to the middle of a bog where, beside an abandoned hearse, we changed our clothes; the picture suffered no damage at all.

As Stanley paints whatever the weather, sometimes on a windswept mountain top in winter or in mid-lake on a bitingly cold spring day, his main object is to keep warm, so a day's painting begins with the dressing. First there is the warm shirt and pullover, covered by a fleece lining from an old coat tied round the waist with a length of string. Next a pair of waterproof pull-ups go over his corduroy trousers. Then come the outer garments and these are strange indeed. An ancient purple rug, reaching below the knees and secured with a rope, goes over an anorak. A tattered blue nylon mac follows, but he is not finished yet, for to keep his head warm is of the utmost importance. A dark blue balaclava, two black berets and an anorak hood complete the outfit. Now he is ready to start a picture.

When Stanley paints he stands quietly, hardly moving, for many hours, with only his eyes and the hand holding the brush busy. He becomes part of the landscape and animals often come close to stare. Once, as he worked on a picture of a Connemara lake, a stoat watched him from a nearby island. With nose quivering, head stretched high, he stood tall on his hind legs but not satisfied with what he saw he decided to investigate further. Diving into the lake he swam swiftly towards the shore. As he drew near, Stanley, not knowing what his intentions were, grew uneasy, coughed and moved his feet; doing a quick turn about the stoat retreated. Another autumn day, in the mountains, as he mixed his colours on his palette he felt a presence behind him. Turning round he saw, only feet away, a very large antlered stag. It was the rutting season and later, as he painted, he heard the stag's roaring echoing over the mountain tops.

To find the perfect subject takes time and much searching and that was what he was doing as he walked through a field of cows. Pausing for a moment, with the animals cropping the grass beside him, he noticed with consternation that one of them wasn't a cow at all but a large nose-ringed bull. Hurriedly leaving the field he climbed through a bramble hedge until he reached the river shore. Three hours later he had a problem; how would he get back to his car without meeting the bull? He solved it by wading through the swiftly flowing river, his canvas held high above his head, while the force of the water nearly swept him off his feet.

But his strangest encounter was with a cock pheasant. One morning as he removed his painting equipment from the boot of the car, an enormous pheasant, his feathers glowing with colour, appeared through a gate from a cornfield. Walking over to Stanley he stood looking at him, then, strutting the length of the car and back, he made his first attack. Taken by surprise, the easel was used to ward off the fierce jab from the sharp beak but when he made his way down to the shore the bird followed, his attacks increasing. He had never had to use his painting equipment as a shield before but now it became a vital means of defence and as the vicious thrusts were parried the creature danced furiously. Crossing a rickety bridge over a stream the pheasant followed. Along the sand they both went and, while the easel was being set up, the pheasant prowled like an angry guard dog. At last he gave up and, with his very long tail held high, set off back the way he had come. We learned later that he had attacked many people; in fact he made a habit of it. He was captured once and put under a wheelbarrow but he leaped out in a rage when someone, unknowingly, removed it. But his reign of terror ended at last when he went into the oven to make a tasty dinner.

The Guinness estate of Lugalla, deep in the Wicklow mountains, is a favourite place for walkers. One day, Stanley, dressed in his usual winter painting outfit, set up his easel a couple of yards inside the entrance gates and began work on a very large, eight-foot canvas. A car passed, coming from the direction of the house a mile away. It stopped on the road below and a man and a woman got out.

'Have you permission to paint here?' they asked him in a not very friendly manner.

'I've painted here many times,' he answered. 'No one has ever objected before.'

The couple drove off but within minutes a jeep arrived and a game warden, with a portable phone, approached him. 'You *can't* paint here,' he said. 'I'll have to ask you to leave.'

'I *must* finish my picture,' Stanley told him. 'I'm only half way through.'

'How would you like it if someone painted in *your* front garden?' the warden replied. Then as Stanley looked around at the rolling mountainside, the acres of heather and gorse, an expression of amazement appeared on the man's face. 'I know you,' he said. 'You're a local clergyman.'

The network of roads running through the forests of County Wicklow make it easy to get lost, and the forest 'curfews' don't help. Once Stanley, with Lir sitting on the back seat, drove four miles into the heart of the woods where he parked the car and walked another mile to his painting site. Some hours later, picture completed, Lir and he retraced their steps and drove back the way they had come. It was early afternoon but already the iron bar, securely padlocked, was across the entrance. Shock and horror! they were locked in. 'I'll try another route,' he thought but soon large rocks and boulders blocked his path. The silence of the forest is often shattered by the noise of chainsaws working but that day not a sound disturbed the stillness, no forester walked the paths or appeared through the trees, the woods seemed quite empty.

Some time later two hikers came down the track and when asked if they knew of any other way out of the forest for a car, they replied, 'You could try this route which goes towards Roundwood.' With Lir looking anxiously over his shoulder, Stanley drove on and on until at last an entrance appeared ahead. But was it open or closed? With great relief they found that the bar was only half way across; just enough room for a small car to squeeze through. As they took the road for Roundwood, Stanley turned to Lir. 'Do you know how lucky you are to be going home?' he said. The dog's happily wagging tail was response enough.

Stanley is totally absorbed when he paints; he rarely thinks of anything else. He and his small boat have been marooned in the mud of an estuary until the tide came in again. On another occasion he and his dog watched in consternation as the same boat, caught by the flow, drifted further and further away; no one was more relieved than the dog when it was retrieved. One late autumn afternoon Stanley was packing up to return home with a finished picture. Carefully holding it and his easel in both hands, he stepped down from the river bank into his nine-foot boat but, misjudging the distance, he landed awkwardly, overbalanced and capsized. Down into the water the boat and he, still clutching picture and easel, went. Fortunately the river at that point was only waist deep but it took all his strength to drag the waterlogged craft half way up the bank, tip out some of the water and bale the rest. An hour later he arrived home with his picture, both sopping wet, but luckily neither were the worse for wear.

Painting out of doors has many hazards. At 5 am on a summer's morning in Connemara the midges are unbelievably vicious. They bite and stick to the paint on the canvas and later each one has to be removed with a pin. Bad weather is always a threat. On a typical West of Ireland day, as Stanley started to paint in the centre of a bog, the clouds descended and when driving rain followed he had no protection from the elements. He became so wet that, returning to the car, he removed his sodden clothes and when a blink of sunlight appeared, draped them over the bonnet and the roof. Waiting for them to dry he sat, stark naked, inside. The last thing he expected was a hoard of tourists on bicycles to appear; nothing had prepared them for the sight of a car festooned with strange garments and a totally naked man inside.

But sometimes Stanley too has strange encounters. On a cold November morning he drove the car over the fields and down to the lake at the upper end of Lough Dan. Parking it under the trees, where it was partly hidden, he began a picture. From the mountain tops came the sound of a helicopter and minutes later it appeared, flying down the length of the lake. Over the partly hidden car, and the painter, it began a hovering descent, the tall white grass flattening as the blades rotated with a tremendous roar. When it was only yards from the ground the door opened and a man in battle dress holding a gun looked out, preparing to jump. The painter, brush in hand, waved. The man grinned broadly, waved back and the helicopter rose, banked steeply and disappeared from sight.

When Stanley conducts a School of Painting he introduces people, often for the first time, to outdoor painting. To feel the sun, the wind, and sometimes the rain, on their faces as they paint is to add a new dimension to their lives. One of his students, who painted outside for the first time, told me that she had never before really looked down into a bog. 'It is beautiful,' she said. 'Now I have God above me and God below my feet.' In the evenings, after his lecture and discussion time, if he has fired people with some of his own enthusiasm and love of nature, he is content.

When Stanley is asked the question, '*Why* do you paint?' His answer is, 'To try and express in some tangible way my emotions of excitement and wonder at the beauties of nature.' He was a student when he first met Michael Farrell, a gentle mystic and Irish painter living in Paris, who told him, 'To me, to paint is to pray.' That is what painting means to Stanley too.

16
Living with Animals

If painting is an important part of Stanley's life, animals are central to mine. The old stables at Annamoe rectory were spooky, with crumbling walls and gaping windows, but I often wondered what they must have been like two hundred years before when they were built. How many horses lived in the stalls, a work animal perhaps and one to pull the trap or for the parson to ride when he visited his parishioners? I could imagine the loft filled with sweet smelling hay and a pile of dung steaming in a corner of the yard. I could almost hear the clatter of hooves on the cobble-stones and the clanking of buckets as the horses were fed. But those stables had been empty for many years and there was a feeling of sadness about the place for something long gone.

I first rode a horse on the two-mile strand at Portstewart in County Derry when I was twelve years old. Huge Atlantic waves roared in on that exposed beach, with spray flying and rivulets of foam curling on to the sand to the shrieks of bathers; swimming there was very exhilarating indeed. Every day during the summer, a string of horses and ponies arrived and stood patiently waiting for customers. A ride of about two hundred yards cost one shilling but I had never experienced anything like it before. Sitting on a high sand-dune I would watch the activity on the strand below until I decided that the right moment had come for my few minutes of heaven. The ride was over almost before it had begun and as I walked home I relived every second.

In Belfast I attended a riding-school once a week with my friends. It took two tram journeys to get there and our excitement rose with every mile. As the horses were led out we would stand, backs to the wall, riding-crops in hands, hearts beating fast, to be 'thrown up' by the ancient bleary-eyed groom. Most of our riding was along roads and we had to pass the tram terminus, twice. It was thrilling when your horse, frightened by the banging and clattering as the vehicle changed direction, went up on the footpath in a cantering shy. Although that establishment called itself a riding 'school' we were given no tuition at all and what we were allowed to do was hightly dangerous – and hard hats were not considered necessary. My parents came to see me mounted, once. Afterwards, to my great disappointment, they didn't mention my riding skills. Not one word about my 'good seat' or my 'nice leg position' was uttered but as we arrived home my mother turned to me and said, 'That was a *very* small horse you were on.'

When Stanley was a final-year divinity student I went again to Sligo for Christmas. On the first day of my holiday we cycled the four miles to Knocknarea where, beside a shed under the shadow of the mountain, we parked our bikes. On opening the door a smell of horse floated out; inside was a bay gelding contentedly munching hay. 'His name is Romper Hero,' Stanley told me. 'He's yours for a week.' Accompanied by Stanley on his bike, I rode along country lanes, over the lower slopes of Knocknarea and down to the wide strand of Culleenamore. His friend Dick, hearing that we had only one horse, lent us a large grey work animal called Seamew so that we could ride together. But Romper Hero was a fast walker while Seamew plodded slowly, so often there was some distance between us as we rode. Splashing along by the pillers on the flats to Coney Island one day, a gun went off close by. Sand flew in all directions as my mount disappeared with me towards the island while the grey, not being fond of fast travel, whirled round and round in tight circles until Stanley's head spun. On my last evening in Sligo that Christmas, with the horses snorting in the frosty air and a full moon rising, we rode home and Stanley told me that he had paid for Romper Hero's hire with a book grant for £10 given to him by the bishop!

When, after leaving Annamoe, we moved to Wicklow a plan began to form in my mind to keep a horse, for there was a two-acre field attached to the rectory. The house was very large, three storeys high, so each week I had someone for a few hours to help me with the housework. But I had a proposition for Stanley. If I did without that ' help' would he pay me so that I could save to buy a horse? He was doubtful at first as I had the family to look after, the telephone and door bell to answer and the parish activities to contend with but, eventually, he agreed.

Two years later I bought Lisa, a five-year-old fourteen-two-hand pony mare with a white face and four white socks. Judith was entering her teens and that summer we would saddle up Lisa in the cool of an evening and, with two of her friends and me on bikes, we sallied forth along the honeysuckle filled Wicklow lanes. The rider changed often but that patient pony tolerated them all. On her second summer with us, my friend Lore lent me her grey mare Dolly so that Judith and I could ride together. On Dolly's last day with us we set off to return her to Annamoe. It was a long journey of twelve miles and as we passed Glenealy, six miles from Wicklow, the sun beat down. Lisa, deciding that she had gone far enough, whipped round and made for home but Judith, using all her riding skills, managed to get her back on course. After a rest of twenty-four hours at Annamoe, we started our trek back. Lore, on Dolly, rode with us to the top of Ballymacrow hill and when we parted I thought that Lisa would refuse to leave her pony friend but to our amazement, without as much as a whinnied 'good-bye', she strode off in the direction of Wicklow.

Lisa was gentle and kind but she missed the company of other horses so a few years later we got a companion for her, a black yearling donkey called Grainne who turned out to be a champion, for she won over fifty rosettes at shows, including that of the Royal Dublin Society. One year, ridden by her little friend Elizabeth, she was runner-up in the All Ireland riding class. Grainne's successes increased her value to much more than the £20 I had paid for her and that fact nearly brought us a disaster. One day two men appeared and leaning over the field gate they watched our animals grazing. The next day they were back and an ancient horse-box was parked not far away. At the garda station they listened carefully to what I had to say, before telling me, 'Those men are donkey thieves.' That night, and for many weeks afterwards, I padlocked all our gates and the stable door and I didn't sleep too well for a long time.

Stallions have a different call to the rich mellow tones of mares. The sound of their neighing can be extremely frightening and that was what I heard, one summer morning, coming from the direction of our field. Rushing out I saw a big piebald stallion pounding up and down outside the fence while on the inside, Lisa, with much tail swishing, was trotting agitatedly. Calling her name I ran towards her and, to my great relief, she came to me. What took place next happened so fast that all I saw was the stallion, now *inside* the field, galloping towards us at full stretch. Self-preservation is a powerful motive. I ran and I never climbed out of a field so fast. Lisa followed me up to the fence, the stallion right behind her, rearing, bucking and screaming, while she landed some hefty kicks on his broad muscular chest.

In the house John heard the commotion and hurried out. 'Don't go into the field,' I shouted. 'You could be killed.' But he did go in and brandishing a stick he somehow managed to chase the stallion away, closing a gate behind him. But the episode wasn't over yet, for while Stanley sped off in the car to search for the owner, John and I patrolled the fence, shouting and waving our arms, as the large creature hurtled towards us, trying to jump in again. The owner, a traveller, wasn't to be found but two girls came to deal with the situation until a young lad appeared to lead the animal away.

Some time later I met the owner of the stallion and while he pleaded ignorance of the whole affair he couldn't resist saying, 'Think of the lovely foal you'd get, Missus.'

It is twenty-eight years since I bought Lisa and she and Grainne are still with me She is in her thirty-fourth year now and the donkey is aged twenty-four. Every morning the two old ladies are waiting for me to let them into their field and every evening they call loudly to hurry me up with their night feed. They spend their days in gentle contentment, quietly grazing together, and at night they stand side by side in the stable. It has been a great privilege to own them and to have had their friendship.

There have been many animals in my life. Some have belonged to me while others, creatures of the wild, have needed my help. It is extremely difficult to succeed with these for it takes time and patience and often they die of shock. My failure to save a baby shell-duck caused me great distress. It was dusk when a young couple came to the rectory with a fluffy little duck wrapped in a handkerchief. As they had walked by the shore, with darkness not far away, they saw a duckling running alone by the water's edge, calling loudly. Thinking that he was lost and not realising that, most probably, the mother was close by they picked him up and brought him to me. Their action, so kindly meant, was a terrible mistake. It was dark by then and too late to return him to his home some miles away. But where were we to put him for the night? We tried a box but he instantly climbed out, so the cage, once used by our canary, seemed the answer. With a feather duster to cuddle into, a dish of chopped sardines, another for water, and the cage covered for warmth, we left him for the night. In the morning he was clamouring to get out. We put him on the sitting-room floor where he ran between Stanley and me, piping a beautiful high-pitched song. When he grew tired he climbed on to our knees. Stanley wrote his Sunday sermon with that delightful little creature snuggled under his pullover. But as day turned to evening the tiny duck became lethargic and when we put him in his cage he was distressed. Twice he went into shock but, cupped in Stanley's warm hands, he revived. At 1 am I was still holding him but he had grown very weak. Half an hour later not even my hot tears could revive him.

Domestic ducks make interesting pets. Not only do they give wonderful eggs but they are amusing, while their gentle quacking is therapeutic. Joanna, brown and white and of no particular breed, was my all-time favourite. She knew her name and would answer me when I called her. Ducks can be nervous creatures but not Joanna; she loved to be held in my arms and stroked, when her quacking would become a gentle croon. I had her for many years but in old age she became ill. When the vet's medication didn't help her I knew, with sadness, that her life was nearly over. But I didn't expect her death to be so violent; one evening I found her mutilated and decapitated body lying beside the duck house. Then I raged in anger and distress at the fox who had done the terrible deed. A week later I walked in the fields and I saw, through a gap in the hedge, a vixen with two tiny cubs. Unaware of us, she sat yawning and relaxed in the sunshine while they played beside her. Then I was able to accept Joanna's death and forgive, for that vixen had a family to feed.

I love all animals but my favourites are dogs. My first dog was an imaginary one, but he was very real to me, and his collar and lead hung at the end of my bed. When I was ten years old I was promised a puppy. Every day I hurried home from school hoping that he would be waiting for me and one day he was. Parked outside our gate was an ancient car, the front door of our house was open and sitting on a newspaper in the hall was a large brown-and-white puppy. Paddy was a four-month-old cocker spaniel, we were told; he grew into an English setter! After he died I had to wait until we moved to Annamoe to have a dog again. Then Jumbo came to us and when his life ended he left a big gap in our home. Cliff and Kem were labrador-red-setter cross puppies with black shiny coats who were very much part of our children's young lives. Sadly Kem died at the age of eight.

Cliff lived for another four years, a highly intelligent animal who understood over one hundred words. He liked to listen to our conversations, turning his head from one of us to the other, until he heard a word that he recognised; then his eyes would brighten and his tail would wag. People in the parish knew him well for every weekday he went with Stanley to church where, lying quietly on the chancel steps, he would greet everyone who came in. He attended the children's services too, going from pew to pew as the boys and girls arrived, to receive pats on the head. The end of Cliff's life was a shock to us, for although he was an old dog he had never lost his zest for living. When he died it was as if a light had gone out of our lives.

For many years I had been troubled by the question, 'Have animals souls? Will we meet them again?' A week after Cliff died, full of sadness I walked in his favourite place and, suddenly, he was with me and I felt peace and joy. And I had my answer: *Yes, animals do have souls.* I wonder now how I could *ever* have doubted it.

Cara was an eight-week-old yellow labrador puppy, the same size as our cat who hated her on sight. Kit, a totally wild snow-white kitten, had been born in the rectory garden and after many months of patience our son Michael and I managed to ' tame ' her but to the end of her seventeen years of life a wild streak remained in her. The winter after she was born we were anxious to introduce her to the house, and to Cliff, but it was with trepidation that we brought her indoors. Trotting jauntily into the kitchen as if she had always lived there, she took one look at Cliff and fell in love. She followed that very large dog everywhere, often terrifying him by jumping out, playfully, from behind doors. When he died she grew thin and disinterested in life, refusing to eat; it took a long time for her to recover. After that she disliked every dog we owned and treated them with great contempt. They all learned to be wary of her sudden tempers.

Cara, grew up into a placid, kind and motherly dog and when Niamh, a tiny terrified stray, came into our lives, she adopted her at once. We didn't mean to have two dogs again but soon we had three! Nooly, a brown-and-white puppy with a woolly coat, strayed into a china shop where, seated amongst the cups and saucers in the window, she watched the passing traffic. The shopkeeper chased her out but she was back in a minute. No one claimed her so that amusing little animal, with mischief dancing from her amber eyes, joined our family of dogs. For the next eight years those three bitches lived, slept, ate and went for walks together and not once, in all that time, did they fight. Occasionally Nooly, in a light-hearted way, tried to oust Cara as top dog in the pecking order. Cara never reprimanded her but would look at me with a shocked expression as if to say, 'Did you see that?' So I would have to do some reprimanding!

Then there was Kizz, who didn't belong to us at all. I first saw her when she was three months old, a tiny yellow labrador puppy owned by our neighbours. Little did I know then just how important she would become in my life. After that first meeting I didn't see her again until a year later when she appeared, nervously, in the rectory garden. She had reason to be afraid; Niamh, fiercely possessive of her home and everything that belonged to it, furiously chased her away. A few days passed and Kizz was back, to be once more subjected to Niamh's aggression. And that became the pattern of Kizz's early association with us. In her own family she had the company of three dogs but for some strange reason she wanted to live with us. In spite of Niamh's hostility she spent most days in our garden and in the evening, when our pets were in the house, she would sit outside forlornly, looking in through the windows. After we pulled the curtains a peep out would often disclose that she was *still* there. It was a most distressing situation.

For *eight* years this pattern continued and then, almost

overnight, everything changed. Niamh died suddenly, Kizz's owners were emigrating, and *she* was refusing to go to her own home at all. One morning we discovered that she had spent the bitterly cold night lying on the concrete outside our back door. That evening I made a bed for her in our small back porch. For a time this arrangement worked but late one evening I opened the back door for a moment. On going to close it I found that Kizz was sitting *inside* the kitchen and her gaze, which was fixed intently on me, seemed to be saying, *'It's time I moved in.'* I *couldn't* resist the appeal in her brown eyes any longer and from that moment, in her mind, she belonged to us. The next day I wrote to her owners in England to ask if she could be ours. I had to wait five long weeks before the reply came but the answer was 'yes'. After all those years Kizz had got her wish and happiness radiated from her. She was my shadow and grew sad if I was away from her even for a short time. Two years passed happily but then to our great sorrow Cara, who was by now an old dog, died.

When Kizz became mine I had thought, 'If I could have her for four years I would be content.' Now she was thirteen years old. Those four years were nearly over and they were not enough. We were in Killarney with Nooly and her when she became ill. Returning home early we paid a visit to the Veterinary College in Dublin where they confirmed our own vet's diagnosis; Kizz had a brain tumour. It was painful to see our lovely dog grow so thin, a shadow of her former self. When she became weak and confused I called our young vet and asked him to put her to sleep. Denis spent a long time examining her and when he had finished he said, 'I have a strong feeling that what you are asking me to do is not right for Kizz.' For five days and nights she lay in her bed, peaceful and quiet and in no pain. When she grew too weak to drink I put drops of water into the corner of her mouth. As I stroked her head, speaking gently to her, I knew that the vet had been right; *this* was the way that Kizz wanted it to be. She slipped away in the early morning of the sixth day. She died with dignity, surrounded by love, but it was a dark dark day for me. After Kizz died, Nooly was without a dog companion for the first time in her life and her loneliness was pitiful. We thought of getting a puppy for her but thirteen-year-old Nooly had arthritis and was getting frail, so we decided against it. She lived for another eight months and then one day she lay down in her bed, gave a little sigh, and was gone. A chapter in our lives had closed.

Now we have a young dog again, a gentle bearded collie called Lir, who runs and jumps and demands walks and loves to go out in our small boat when, leaning over the bow, he looks deep into the rippling water or up into the sky to bark at the flying gulls. Then, for fun, we call him Captain Bleary Leary! So the whole cycle, which will end in such pain for us, has begun again. Dogs live too short a time. In a few quick years they are gone, but to have shared their lives is the most enriching and rewarding of experiences. During the five long days that I spent with Kizz as her life was ebbing to a close, I thought of how she had tried to walk with me through the dappled sunshine of a Killarney wood, where the deer came down to the lake to drink, and I wrote these lines in dedication:

To Kizz

A man came over the mountains to where a deer lay dying beside a pool dark and still. No fear was in her eyes or in her heart. Seeing her lying there he raised his gun.

'I'll finish this,' he said, 'for I know best.'

Man and deer alone in a twilight world. As he looked into those calm eyes, the hunter paused. 'Perhaps not yet,' he murmured. 'Perhaps not yet.' And putting his gun away, he left.

17

A School in the Parish

As we entered our second year in Annamoe an idea was germinating in Stanley's mind. 'We need a school,' he said. A school is the life-blood of a parish, and the benefits are not only educational but social, for it draws the people together, especially in scattered country areas. In the 150 square miles of our parish there was no Church of Ireland school and the children had to travel great distances to be educated. So Stanley called a meeting of all the parishioners to discuss it. Derralossary hall was packed that evening and everyone agreed that a school would be a wonderful asset. And so Stanley began the long arduous business of negotiating with the Department of Education, travelling regularly to Dublin for meetings. It took two intensive years before he at last received the go-ahead. A letter from the Inspector stated, 'I can find no diriment impediment to the founding of a school.' The Department had sanctioned it at last.

The business of fund raising began in earnest, with everyone joining in enthusiastically. The only hall in the parish was at Derralossary and this basic structure was to be extended for the school. In the spring of 1960 the site was cleared and work began. Lavatories and a tiny kitchen were built, a playground laid and fenced. Much of the work was done voluntarily and Stanley and his team dammed a stream two hundred yards away and put in a second-hand Ram pump. Then the heavy job of digging a trench was undertaken and a water-pipe was laid. The final painting of the inside walls of the building was completed and, to great rejoicing, the school was ready.

That September Stanley advertised for a teacher but there

was no rush of applicants; in fact only one person replied. She came to the rectory to be interviewed and stayed with us for the night. She was middle-aged and motherly and fulfilled all the Department of Education's requirements. Stanley appointed her. Next a transport scheme with a suitable vehicle and a driver had to be organised, for the fifteen pupils would come from a large, scattered area. This had to be funded by the parish – in those days there was no free Goverment school transport – so Stanley began a round of speaking to various societies who aided isolated schools. He pleaded his case to the Island and Coast Society, the Church Education Society and the Diocesan Board of Education amongst others. Fund raising in the parish began again.

Everything was set for the opening in January when a totally unexpected set-back occured. Two days before the school was due to start Stanley received a phone call from a parishioner who had learned that our teacher had no intention of taking up her post with us and was already looking for an appointment elsewhere. We had a real crisis on our hands. But the school *did* open on the Monday morning and during the first week of its life Stanley taught the fifteen pupils himself, as well as having many desperate consultations with the Department of Education and the Church of Ireland Training College in Dublin to find a teacher. By the end of the week he had the name of a student who would qualify for temporary teaching but she lived in County Donegal.

'I'll phone her immediately,' he said.

'She's not on the phone,' came the reply.

'Then I'll go to Donegal and find her,' Stanley answered.

At 5 am in the cold darkness of a Saturday morning, he left the rectory for Dublin where our friend Jack joined him, and together they set off on the two-hundred-mile trip to Lifford. After four hours driving they arrived to find that the girl they were seeking wasn't there. On they went to Port-na-blagh where, to their great relief, they found her. Some hours into the journey home, Mina, a second-year student at the Church of Ireland College of Education, unwittingly dropped a bomb-shell. Stanley, it appeared, had been given the name of the wrong girl; it should have been Mina's *older* sister, also a student at the College of Education, whom they should have contacted!

On Monday morning Mina started teaching while Stanley made yet another journey to Dublin to plead with the Department of Education to let her stay. Permission was granted, but only for two weeks. And that became the pattern of Mina's time with us; every fortnight the Department's permission had to be sought again. In the end she was allowed to teach at Derralossary for a whole year before returning to her studies in Dublin. Although she was only eighteen years old and still a student she was a splendid teacher and the pupils loved her. She lived with us at the rectory and it was nice to have someone young in the house. Although she must have missed her friends, and the lack of a social life, she never complained. We were sad when she left us.

The school made a huge difference in the life of our parish, for now we had proper facilities for sales and social functions. The first concert played to a packed house, with every class taking part. It was a long performance but no one minded that. The Christmas party was a great event, not only for the children but their parents and grandparents as well. Judith was one of those first fifteen pupils and at last she had friends. Among them were Noeleen and her young brother Mervyn who had come to live in Annamoe. Bobby came from Laragh, and every afternoon when the school minibus, driven by kind reliable Paddy McCoy, brought Judith home, Bobby came with her to play. As the minibus appeared up the avenue John would rush excitedly to the front door to join in the games.

Everything in the school ran smoothly except for some day to day problems and one of these was with the water supply. Every morning Stanley drove to the school to check it and often the flow had stopped. Then, taking off his jacket and rolling up his shirt-sleeves, he would kneel down on the frozen earth and plunge his arm elbow deep into the icy water to free the blockage. But he had another worry; the Department of Education insisted that the average school attendance should not drop below ten pupils. In the winter there were always some children off sick and during Judith's first year there she caught every cough, cold and ear infection that was going. 'She can't be sick *again*,' Stanley would say in despair. It was a bone of contention between us and I couldn't wait for the holidays to come.

Over the years Stanley seemed destined to be involved in education for when we moved to Wicklow he taught in five different schools each week. He built the new Glebe school on Church Hill, which was followed by the new Nun's Cross school in Killiskey Parish. When the East Glendalough Secondary Comprehensive was planned for County Wicklow he found a site for it in Wicklow town and was deeply involved in every stage of its progress, being appointed to the first Board of Management, with all meetings being held in Wicklow rectory during the first two years.

A few months after Derralossary school opened Judith was going to be five years old and we were planning a birthday party for her, something she had never had before. We discussed the food, the colour of the jelly, the birthday cake and the games to play. Four school friends were invited, including Mervyn, and not wanting to leave out his eleven-year-old sister, Noeleen, we asked her too. We decorated the sitting-room with balloons and carried the big kitchen table into the study where Kathleen, whose little sister was also coming, and I laid it for tea. Judith wore a red velvet dress for the occasion and John had a new pullover. When all was ready Stanley drove to Roundwood and Laragh to collect the guests. The children were shy as the party began but soon their laughter echoed round the room as Hunt the Thimble,

Musical Bumps and Pass the Parcel were played. The food was eaten, the birthday-cake candles blown out, the crackers pulled, the treasure hunt for tiny gifts had taken place, and all too soon the party was over. Stanley loaded the guests into his car and set off with them on the homeward journey while Kathleen and I surveyed the debris. It had been a good party.

Ten miles away at the far end of the parish there lived a family with two big boys, soon to leave Derralossary for secondary school. As Stanley left church on the following Sunday the boys' mother was waiting for him.

'I hear you had a party at the rectory,' she said.

'We did,' Stanley replied. 'It was Judith's fifth birthday.'

'I hear the whole of Derralossary school was invited, except my lads,' continued the mother.

'Four little ones were invited,' Stanley answered, '*certainly* not the whole school.'

'*That's* not what I heard,' stormed the woman. 'I suppose we're not good enough.' Stanley was very taken aback, but she wasn't finished yet. 'Is *Noeleen* what you call a little one?' she raged. 'Discrimination, that's what it is. You can tell missus I won't forget this.' And after that, any time we met, she refused to speak to me.

I learned something from that very hurtful experience, althought it wasn't until later years that I fully understood it. No matter *what* a clergyman's wife does, or *how* good her intentions are, she will often be criticised or misunderstood by someone.

In Annamoe the summer was over, the flies and midges had gone, the days were mellow. As we walked down the avenue the children's feet scuffled and kicked the dead leaves and a golden shower flew high into the air. The hedgerows were heavy with blackberries, which Jumbo carefully nipped off with his teeth, while our hands and lips were stained purple as we too ate the ripe fruit. School had started again. Once more it was harvest time and we were decorating our churches. The children of the parish brought offerings of fruit, flowers and vegetables which they placed under the pulpits, as the singing of the familiar hymns rang out:

> Come ye thankful people, come,
> Raise the song of harvest home,
> All is safely gathered in.
> Ere the winter storms begin.

Archbishop Simms was our harvest preacher that year, and as we entertained him in the rectory before the service, Stanley poured glasses of his strong home-made cider. 'Ah,' the archbishop said, as he took a sip of the pale gold liquid, 'I think this is something I should drink *after* I have preached and not before!'

Cecil too made cider in his Sligo rectory and one evening the sound of loud explosions came from the basement. Not knowing what to expect he hurried to investigate, to find that some of the bottles of cider had blown up.

18
Camp-fires in the Dark

One year before we left for our two weeks' holiday in Sligo, Stanley received a letter from Guy, Scout Leader of the Rathfarnham Troop, asking if the company could camp on the rectory land for a week in August. The select vestry had to be consulted, and also the farmer who grazed his cattle there but, to our delight, permission was granted. Stanley had been a scout and I a girl guide and we had both camped often. I loved camping even though most of my memories are of the rain. Of trying to light a fire with damp wood so that we could cook breakfast. Of rain trickling down our necks, splashing over cold bare legs and filling our gum boots. The smell of damp tents as we put our groundsheets and home-made sleeping-bags down on the soggy grass at night. But in spite of all that the fun was ' mighty'!

My very first camp was on a private estate overlooking Strangford Lough in Northern Ireland. On the second morning I wakened to the sound of a boat's engine and opening the tent-flap I looked out. The sun had just risen and a shaft of golden light caught the bow of the boat as it crossed the lough to Portaferry. But the promise of that day didn't last; later heavy rain poured down and we had to be evacuated to the safety of a barn in the night. It was exciting climbing up a rickety ladder to the loft above and snuggling in among the bales of hay as the rain hammered on the corrugated roof but the following morning we were disappointed to learn that the camp was being abandoned and we all had to go home.

Summer holiday over, in Annamoe we were waiting for the scouts to arrive. The excitement was great when, one morning, cars laden with boys and equipment drove up the avenue and the fields rang with the sound of young voices and of tent-pegs being hammered into the ground. The site was beside the river and near the monkey-puzzle and from the rectory windows we could watch the camp being set up. When all was in order we were invited on a tour of inspection and that was when we met scout leader Guy, and his second in command Ian. As we were escorted round the camp on that summer's afternoon we were impressed by everything we saw. The store tent with its food carefully stacked and the daily menus neatly written out, the first-aid tent set up, the patrols organised and already at work. During that week we watched the scouts playing Rounders, running races, and going about their daily duties. In the evenings, when the midges were bad, they covered their heads with towels and sweaters to stop them biting. On their last night they had a camp-fire. In the darkness as sparks shot skyward, the boys sang lustily, their faces illuminated by the leaping flames.

Once, round a camp-fire, my guide friends and I had told ghost stories. Outside the circle of light the darkness was black, with rustlings coming from the wood behind us. As our tale reached its chilling climax, one of the guides gave an unearthly shriek as she pointed into the dark beyond the fire. Our story-telling came to an abrupt end and the poor girl was led away sobbing and hysterical. Later that night, as we closed our tent-flaps and climbed into our sleeping-bags, more than one of us hid our heads in fear wondering just *what* our companion had seen, for the shriek she gave was far more terrifying than any ghost story. After that, tales of the supernatural were strictly banned by the leaders.

As that first scout camp at Annamoe ended we watched sadly as the tents came down, the equipment was packed away and the site carefully cleaned. As the last car disappeared down the avenue, taking the boys home, silence again descended over the fields and the river. That August the weather had been good but the following year, as the scouts arrived, the rain fell from a grey sullen sky. Day after day it poured, the ground turned to mud, the trees dripped moisture and the river was in spate. We offered the use of the rectory basement and the cloakroom off the hall with its wash-hand-basin and toilet. Both were gratefully accepted. The boys came to the house in orderly groups, well behaved and polite, while in the basement long lines of wet clothes dripped on to the stone floors. Towards the end of the week the leaders asked us, 'Could we cook on the old range, would it be safe?' A consultation was held, the large black stove was examined and a fire was lit. It worked perfectly. Then we received an invitation. The scouts invited us to dinner on their last evening.

All that day there was great activity. Strange bumpings and bangings could be heard below while the smell of cooking wafted under the basement door. At seven o'clock, as we made our way down the creaking staircase, Stanley had a joke to play. Wearing a Boys' Brigade cap, from his days as their chaplain in Clontarf, a small cane tucked under his arm, he strode into the basement calling, 'Senior Service, of course.' A roar of indignation rose from the assembled scouts. What an insult to put the Boys' Brigade above the Scout Association! and Stanley was nearly evicted. But as we all sat down to dinner together, he was forgiven. In the basement a transformation had taken place; in one of the dark and gloomy rooms a long table had been constructed and candle-light flickered. The orderly patrol served steaming bowls of soup, followed by roast chicken, potatoes and vegetables. As the meal ended Ian and the cook patrol appeared, their faces flushed from the heat of the ancient range. It was an evening to remember.

Those scout camps were highly organised and run with great efficiency and when they were over the only evidence that they had taken place was the flattened grass where the tents had been pitched. But that autumn Stanley was astonished, and very upset, to receive a solicitor's letter on behalf of the farmer, a parishioner, who rented the land from the parish at an extremely low rate, stating that he did not want the camp there in future. To our great disappointment, for their visit had been the highlight of our summer, the scouts never came again.

Through scouting, Guy and Ian became our friends and have remained so ever since. Ian has travelled the world, teaching in China and Africa. Guy too was a teacher and when he was studying for his degree at Trinity College he had an extraordinary experience. It was 1959 and World Refugee Year. Guy's room in Trinity had, like those of the other students, no telephone, but unaccountably he began to feel a strong urge to apply for one. The waiting-list for a phone in Dublin was about two years but, to his amazement, *his* was installed in *two weeks*. A few days later, as he sat in his room studying, the newly installed phone rang. A well-known lady author was on the line. 'I have just read your letter in the newspaper,' she said. 'I think it is a splendid idea to collect Christmas presents for refugee children and I would like to help with your campaign.' Guy was stunned as he hadn't written any letter to any newspaper or organised any campaign. Someone, it seemed, was playing a hoax on him.

That evening, as he walked by the River Liffey, the sun was setting through a mist over the roof tops and he had a sudden vision of a plane taking off from Dublin on its way to Stuttgart in Germany, where the displaced persons' camps were situated. He knew then, with utter certainty, what he had to do. As he began to set up the project many volunteers came forward to help him, for the idea had caught people's imagination. It snowballed and gained momentum as business firms donated gifts. Guy worked tirelessly and the phone in his room rang day and night. Just before Christmas he chartered a plane, filled it to capacity with presents and left Dublin for Germany. In the camps at Stuttgart, as he helped to distribute the gifts, he found that although his

German was poor he could converse easily. That Christmas was made a happier one for hundreds of refugee children because of Guy's initiative and drive and the kindness and hard work of many people.

Living in very old houses it is easy to imagine supernatural happenings but what I once heard in the rectory wasn't imagined at all. Our friend Jack was staying with us and as we sat chatting by the fire, a door in the basement below slammed loudly and heavy footsteps crossed the flagged floor of the old kitchen. Whoever was down there hadn't come from outside the house for I knew that all the basement windows were heavily barred and the oak back door was bolted top and bottom. Jack heard the footsteps too because he paused in mid-sentence. Stanley heard nothing at all.

I found that episode in Annamoe rectory scary but it wasn't as frightening as John's experience not long ago in a County Wicklow cottage. The well known Bel-Air Hotel and Riding-School, a few miles north of Wicklow town, is owned by the Freeman family. Originally the estate, known as Cronroe, belonged to the Parsons family. Early in the eighteenth century Viscount Rosse sold the estate to Sir John Eccles, whose son built the original house, and it remained in that family for nearly 150 years. Justin Casement, a cousin of Irish patriot, Sir Roger Casement, was the next owner and when it burned down, towards the end of the nineteenth century, he built the present house. When he was a child Roger Casement stayed there often – his signature can be seen on a wall in an upstairs room – and as a student, at Trinity College, he gave Cronroe as his home address. In 1934 the house and estate were sold to an American who changed its name to Bel-Air. Three years later it was bought by Tim and Bridie Murphy and it has remained in that family ever since; Fidelma Freeman is their daughter.

Bel-Air is home not only to the Freeman family, but to numerous ghosts, all friendly I am told, although some people on entering the building beat a hasty retreat. A diviner once stood directly under the lights in the centre of the large entrance hall and claimed that that was the exact spot where all the supernatural activity is generated. Fidelma, who has lived happily with these 'presences' all her life, says that she feels that they all spring from some happening there before the present house was built.

Some years ago John rented a cottage on the estate. He made it into a cosy home with colourful wall-hangings, wood carvings and other treasures from his travels abroad, though one thing that puzzled him was that the wooden floors were always cold, even in hot weather. It was some weeks after he moved in that the noises began.

One evening, as he sat alone, he heard scratching on the glass of both the front and the back doors as if a key was being put into the lock. On going to investigate he found that there was no one there. Feeling uneasy, he played loud music but even over the throbbing beat he could hear the scratching. He was in bed when he first heard the footsteps circling his room and later they sounded in the living-room too. One November night he returned home after midnight, and on entering the cottage the atmosphere felt strange and the air icy. He went to bed quickly but found it hard to sleep. Some hours later he heard horses' hooves and, thinking that the riding-school animals were loose, he went outside to investigate, but the night was totally silent and very dark with no moon. Back in bed the sound of hooves came again, closer this time, as if many horses were passing and he heard plainly the snorting of their nostrils. Then, in the distance, the hunting-horn sounded twice. Dawn was a long time coming and it was only when the grey light crept through the curtains that he slept. When John rented that cottage he didn't know that it was haunted but he learned that some of the local people would never pass it after dark and that one winter's evening, two horses, returning home tired after a long journey, absolutely refused to pass the cottage even though it was on the direct route back to their stables.

19
Another Life

It was January, a cold and miserable month. Derralossary school was one year old, the number of pupils increasing, its future secure. Mina had left us to continue her studies in Dublin and our new teacher, Maud, had arrived. It was our fifth winter in Annamoe, and as Stanley drove Maud and Judith to school each morning the car skidded and slipped on the icy road. Judith, having picked up every virus that was going at school, brought them all home to John. Attending to the children in the middle of the night was an ordeal for, again, the house was freezing. Often, as I put my feet out of bed on those bitter mornings, I longed to curl up and sleep and sleep, especially now that I was expecting another baby.

Seven times that winter Dr Joe Conway travelled from Wicklow to visit the children. As his car appeared up the avenue, the child who was not sick would call, 'Doctor's coming,' for his arrival was always an event.

Judith was two years old the first time that Joe attended her. While we waited for him to arrive she sat in her cot flushed with a temperature, a large green hat with a feather on her head, white gloves on her hands and a handbag over her arm; Judith loved dressing up. As the doctor and I walked up the stairs together I told him, 'She's very shy.' When we entered the room Joe looked at the tiny girl dressed in her finery and a slow smile spread over his face. 'I like your hat,' he said and Judith, who didn't like strange men, smiled sweetly back at him.

Joe was our doctor for thirty-eight years and we owe him a great debt of gratitude for the way he cared for us. In Annamoe his arrival was always a comfort and a relief for, living in that remote place, it was worrying when the children were ill. Joe's practice in Wicklow, which he shared with his mother Benny, was a busy one and yet he never failed to come when we needed him, even in the worst of weather. In ice and in snow his car would drive carefully up the avenue. His Volkswagen beetle was blue but I always remember it as orange, a bright beacon of hope.

I had one other source of help when the children were ill or if there was a problem; I would reach for my copy of *Baby and Child Care* by Dr Benjamin Spock. I found his reasoning and gentle advice practical, well balanced and sympathetic to both mother and child. Later it became unfashionable to praise Dr Spock; he was laughed at and derided for his ideas, sent to prison for his political beliefs and, more recently, accused of being a bad parent. I have often regretted that I didn't write to that poor man to tell him how much he helped a young mother living in a lonely rectory in Ireland. I still have his book, old and battered now and repaired with sellotape, and occasionally I open it, read a little, and relive those early days.

The highlight of the week, for the children and me, was my parents' visits on Sunday afternoons. Standing at the sitting-room windows we would watch for the black Morris Minor to appear up the avenue when the children, running to the front door, would call excitedly, 'Nana and Papa are here.' A box of groceries, to help us through the week, would be carried in and sometimes my mother brought warm vests, ladybird pyjamas or some other articles of clothing which she knew the children needed. One winter there was a new coat for Judith which my mother had made herself. The disappointment was great on those Sundays that the weather was too severe for them to come.

But what I missed most, during our time in Annamoe, was not having a friend, some young woman to talk to and laugh with. It can be difficult to have close friendships in a parish because the line between being your friend and being your husband's parishioner is thin. When you have been hurt or disillusioned by something you can't really unburden yourself to them. Sometimes friendships are even watched with suspicion. 'They're very much *in* with the rectory,' is said disapprovingly. A clergyman of our aquaintance and his very young wife moved to a parish where they were warmly welcomed. One couple in particular was most friendly and helpful. But things changed when the rector introduced 'new ideas', for some people, including this couple, objected. His young wife was bewildered to discover that she too had been included in their censure.

One morning, when spring had at last arrived, Stanley cycled to Laragh for a service of Holy Communion and on his way home he passed a young man, a stranger, mending a fence. Stopping to speak to him Stanley learned that he was German and that he had bought the derelict Laragh House Hotel and was going to farm the land.

'Someone has cut my fence,' he said, indicating the gap in the wire.

'That has always been a right of way,' Stanley answered.

'Then l will leave it unfenced,' he replied.

Back home, Stanley told me of his meeting with Adolf. 'He has a wife and two small children,' he said.

That very afternoon I saw a young woman pushing a pram, a little girl by her side, coming up the rectory avenue. It was Adolf's wife Lore, and their daughters Margaret and baby Christine. Lore spoke little English and I knew no German but we had the common language of motherhood. When she left that afternoon we walked together down the avenue with the children running ahead.

'I'm expecting a baby,' I told her.

'Are you sick?' she asked.

'A little,' I replied.

She nodded, understanding. That friendship made all the difference to my life and at last the children and I had somewhere to go on our walks as the Baders lived close to

Annamoe. Their land stretched up the hillside above the village, much of it covered by gorse and bracken, but over the years Adolf reclaimed it to provide grazing for hundreds of sheep. Deer come down from the mountains to roam freely on his farm and close to the house, which he has built on the site of the old hotel. To see them drinking from the lake beyond the lawn at dusk and watch them, only yards away, was a constant delight.

It was to be our last summer in Annamoe, although we didn't know it at the time, and we had many visitors. The first to arrive were Stanley's brothers, Denis and Keeble, with their wives and children. Denis, the eldest of the family, went into milling after he left school and worked all over the world before settling with his wife Christa and their five children in New Zealand. Keeble has spent his life farming in Zimbabwe and still lives there with his wife Mavis and daughter Sally; their elder daughter Susanne is married and lives in Cape Town in South Africa.

Next to visit us that summer was twelve-year-old Philip, Joan and Cecil's eldest child and my godson, a popular cousin with Judith and John. Early each morning, with the dew still on the grass, they hurried out to the garden to catch rabbits! Holes were dug, camouflaged with leaves and grass, while the three 'trappers' hid close by. 'There they are,' they whispered to each other as the wild rabbits hopped about in the fields, quite unaware of what their fate was meant to be. The 'game' was played for three days until Philip went home to Sligo but Judith and John continued to check the 'traps' daily until, to their disgust, Stanley filled in the holes.

In August my sister Ethne, her husband Paddie and their small son Timothy (who would become a clergyman many years later) spent a day with us. Ethne was pregnant too and her baby, Christopher, was born that autumn two days before Michael. Paddie was a captain in the British Army and he met Ethne when his regiment, the Royal Regiment of

Artillery, was stationed at Hollywood in County Down. By a strange coincidence Paddie's uncle, Dick, had been our rector in Belfast. As children we had been afraid of him and when he called at our house I would run upstairs in case he asked me to say my catechism. In church he was formidable, giving the choir-boys withering looks if they knocked over a book or scuffled their feet. Even the curate was sometimes included in his displeasure. Joan sang in the robed choir but Ethne and I sat at the very front of the packed church with our father. As the rector entered the pulpit his gaze would travel over the large congregation. 'I will start my sermon when *all* the coughing has stopped,' he announced severely one Sunday. Amazingly it did stop, for after that only a brave person would have dared to give even a snuffle during his twenty-five minutes of preaching. One hour and forty-five minutes would pass each Sunday before we were released from the service. It was only when he was preparing us for Confirmation that my friends and I discovered, to our amazement, that he was human and great fun. When he became Ethne's uncle-in-law she told us that he was the nicest and kindest of men.

It was September again and in Annamoe Stanley was having school problems. Maud had left us and after much searching a kindly, retired school principal, full of drive and enthusiasm, was found as a temporary teacher. The bright spot was that the plans for a teacher's residence were approved by the Department of Education and building had begun. At home we were having problems too; Judith had mumps. My baby was due in three weeks and as the days passed I waited anxiously for a swelling to appear under *my* ears, for I had never had mumps. Luckily I escaped but on the last day of the quarantine, when Stanley had taken me to the maternity hospital in Dublin, the telltale swelling appeared on John's face. Once more my parents came to the rescue and nursed him. At the Rotunda hospital a porter led me to a lift and as

Stanley placed my case inside he was told, 'You must leave your wife now, husbands aren't allowed any further.' The grid door clanged shut, the lift slowly ascended and Stanley disappeared from my sight. It was a lonely moment.

Michael's birth was easy and over quickly. As he slept in his cot by my bed I would look out from my window, high up on the top floor of the hospital, over the roof tops of Dublin to the mountains beyond, and down to the staff tennis-court below. As I watched the doctors and nurses playing I longed to join them, for tennis was my favourite sport. The evocative sound of racquet on ball brought back nostalgic memories.

My first tennis lessons took place on the quiet road outside our Belfast house with my father. 'Swing your arm,' he would say as he knocked balls to me. 'Try again. That's better,' he encouraged. 'Not so *hard,*' he would call as I sent the ball whizzing past him. But it was during the war when we lived in Portstewart that I had my real introduction to the game and it wasn't a success. Seven miles away was the country parish of Ballyrashane. The rectory, across a winding lane from the small church, was old and picturesque with virginia-creeper covered walls and a tennis-court in the grounds. The rector and his three sons were fanatical about the game and summer activity centered round the tennis-court. Joan and Ethne were invited to play but at eleven years old I was only a spectator for tennis there was serious stuff. The sunken court was reached by a path through the rockery, while in the wooden summer-house the guests, dressed in immaculate whites, waited their turn to play. The games were fast and furious, the standard high, and to the low thud of the ball the call of 'Fault,' 'Love fifteen,' 'Deuce,' 'Good shot,' rang out. At four o'clock the rector's wife called everyone to tea in the dining-room where faded red blinds were half pulled to keep out the low afternoon sun, but often play didn't stop, for a set being battled out on the court had to be finished. It was at one of those tennis parties that Joan met Cecil. That afternoon I sat in the summer-house with them as they waited their turn for a game. I had no idea that I might be in the way; and it was only when I lost interest in their conversation that I left them

Though I loved walking in the large garden full of flowers, trees and bird song, someone must have thought I was bored; one day I was asked if I had ever played tennis. Thinking of the times my father had given me lessons on the road outside our house, I answered, 'Yes.' A racquet was found for me and for the first time I walked on to a court. The ball came towards me and I swung my racquet as I had been taught to do. To my surprise, and horror, I missed completely. 'You're too close to the net,' someone called. I moved back and tried again. And again. And again. Sometimes I did hit that unpredictable white object but it never cleared the net. Once, by some extraordinary feat, I sent it flying right out of the court and over the high wire fence. That was the worst crime of all. Then my partner took charge of the game and, while I stood idle, he leaped and ran and smashed and volleyed until, single-handed, he had won. After that I went back to being a spectator.

I did learn to play tennis and as a teenager I played all summer long on the courts at Ben Madigan beneath Cave Hill. Stanley played tennis too and we had games during that first summer in Sligo. Often, in Annamoe, I thought with regret of the forgotten tennis-court in the front field which the bullocks had ploughed up with their trampling feet and obliterated.

20
Snow in the Mountains

Michael was ten days old when we returned to the rectory in mid October. Another winter lay ahead of us but strangely, with the coming of this baby, I felt a new hope. The silence of the countryside didn't seem so deep or the darkness so black. Maybe I had got used to Annamoe. Four weeks later Stanley christened him in Derralossary Church, while a damp mist swirled down from the mountains, covering the ancient graves and the twisted thorn bushes. Back in the rectory we piled logs on the fire as our small party of guests arrived and Jack, our friend from Dublin, placed a big silver tablespoon in the baby's tiny hand. Michael's christening seemed to mark a turning-point in our lives. The following Sunday, nominators from the joint parishes of Wicklow and Killiskey appeared in church. Not long afterwards Stanley was offered the rectorship of this large parish on the east coast.

On a bright November day we drove the eleven miles to Wicklow to meet the glebe wardens and to see the rectory, a three-storeyed house with six bedrooms, three attic rooms, numerous living-rooms, sculleries, pantries and a big cheerful kitchen, all in good repair. To our delight there was no basement. 'We're putting an all-night burning grate in the dining-room,' the glebe wardens told us. 'You'll need the extra heat for the children.' From a bedroom window we looked out at the sheltered garden. There were apple-trees on the lawn, rhododendrons, a copper beech, an ancient summer-house, all surrounded by deep high hedges, a perfect place for children to play. The inspection over we stood outside the house with the sun shining on the scarlet autumn leaves of the virginia creeper. We could see traffic on the road but the sound was muffled because a two-acre field lay between it and the rectory. 'You'll be very welcome here,' the glebe wardens said as we all shook hands.

Wicklow and Killiskey parishes wanted Stanley quickly for they had been without a rector for some time, so the Institution date was set for early December, barely a month away. Those weeks rushed by with so much to do. As I sorted, discarded and packed, the baby, to my relief, slept peacefully. But it was a hectic time. One evening in Derralossary school a farewell presentation was made to Stanley. There were gifts for me too and standing on the tiny platform I made my first speech.

When clearing out the basement we had made an unexpected discovery. Buried under piles of clothes for the parish jumble-sale we found an almost full case of wine. Then we remembered where it had come from. A few years earlier, a parishioner, one of the jet set, arrived at the rectory door with a large wooden box. 'Something for you to sell at the fête,' she said. When she had gone Stanley opened the box – inside were one dozen bottles of wine. He looked at me aghast; there was no possible way in the 1950s that we could sell wine at a country parish function. Not knowing what to do with it we put it in the basement and forgot all about it.

'What on earth are we to do with that?' Stanley said.

'We could drink a little,' I answered.

'We could *not*,' Stanley replied. 'It wasn't meant for us.'

Then we thought of a continental friend who liked the occasional glass of wine, so putting the box in the car Stanley went to see him. He was back shortly to tell me that our friend would only take a few bottles.

'We could give some to other people,' I suggested.

'And what would the giver think if she discovered we were providing people all round the parish with her wine,' Stanley replied.

So the bottles stayed in the basement for another few weeks but the day before we were due to leave Annamoe, they and Stanley disappeared. When he returned he was carrying a spade. 'I've solved the problem,' he said. 'I've buried them!' Over the years we have often wondered if those nine bottles of wine are still there, perhaps now under the present owner's swimming-pool or his beautifully laid out Japanese garden. Those of our friends who know the story don't let us forget what we did. 'Sacrilege,' they say shaking their heads. But who knows; perhaps in a hundred years' time someone will find them and enjoy some very fine vintage wine.

On the morning of 4 December we crept downstairs early, trying not to waken the children, so that we could make a good start while they were still asleep. Later, as I bathed and fed Michael, the removal van arrived. Judith and John ran excitedly from room to room until they were banished to the safety of the kitchen. In the afternoon I went upstairs for the last time. Standing in our bedroom, with all the furniture gone, I remembered the first time I had seen Annamoe rectory. How, in the early morning sunshine, I had looked out of the windows at the fields and hedges stretching to the horizon, with the river glinting through the trees. So much had happened in those five and a half years and as the memories flooded in, I turned quickly and hurried downstairs. The house echoed with the hollow sound of empty rooms and the tramping of feet on bare boards when the children and I left for the Baders' house.

It was dusk when the removal van set off for Wicklow and Stanley came for us. 'We must hurry,' he said. 'Snow is forecast.' The rectory was in darkness when we drove up the avenue to collect Jumbo, anxiously waiting in the empty kitchen. He bounded into the front of the car while the children and I crowded together in the back. Michael, oblivious to what was happening, lay asleep in my arms while

Judith nursed her doll and John his teddy. Stanley locked the heavy front door with the large iron key. He drove slowly through the first gate, closing it behind him, and we could hear the roar of the river close by. The bullocks, caught for a moment in the headlights, galloped off, their breath steaming in the bitter night air. I looked back at the dark silent house. The outer gate was opened and closed.

We were crossing the humpback bridge when the first flakes drifted down. As we passed Glendinnings' corner and Patsy Duffy's cottage already the three street lamps of Annamoe were blurred by the falling snow. Up the Wicklow road we went, past Tomriland crossroads, to Ballymacrow hill where the road was white. On the descent from the plateau to the lowlands the snow eased and when we reached the bottom of that steep hill it had stopped altogether. Ahead we could see the lights of Wicklow twinkling in the dark. As we drove towards them a new chapter in our lives had begun.

Epilogue

One more rector followed Stanley at Annamoe after which the parish was divided up and the rectory sold. Calary Church on the bog was given into the care of Newcastle and Newtownmountkennedy parish, while St John's in Laragh was incorporated into the parish of Rathdrum and Glenealy. Ancient Derralossary, with only a handful of parishioners, was closed but the school continued on.

It is thirty-five years since we left Annamoe. Now it is the home of the rich and the famous. A film director lives at the rectory, a traditional musician of world renown has a house in the village, while a well-known actor owns Castle Kevin. The humpback bridge over the Avonmore River was washed away in a storm and has been replaced by a modern structure. The wooden gate to the rectory is gone while an electronic one has taken its place. The derelict gate lodge disappeared long ago. There are bungalows on the road to Laragh.

Yet little has changed. In the village the pretty white cottages, with their flower-filled gardens, and the shop selling groceries are still there. In the grounds of the old rectory the dark spiky monkey-puzzle-tree stands tall, while in spring catkins bloom by the river and primroses stud its banks. The house, seen from a distance, looks much the same. The silence is as deep as it was all those years ago, disturbed only by the sound of the river as it travels, green and silver, ever flowing, through that beautiful and peaceful valley.

After thirty years as rector of Wicklow and Killiskey parishes Stanley has retired. He and Vera live in a small bungalow overlooking the beautiful Broadlough lake with the

Sugerloaf, the Wicklow hills and the sea in the distance. There they get their inspiration for painting and writing. Vera is chairperson of the local branch of the Irish Guide Dogs for the Blind and is active in the Society for the Prevention of Cruelty to Animals. She has written four books for children: *The Adventures of Henry & Sam & Mr Fielding; Henry & Sam & Mr Fielding: Special Agents; Fionuala the Glendalough Goat; Fionuala the Glendalough Goat Goes West.*

Judith has a PhD in Social Anthropology from the University of Cambridge and is also an occupational therapist. She divides her time between Nepal, Cambridge, Ireland and Switzerland, where she is currently a Post-Doctoral Fellow at the University of Zurich.

John is a landscape gardener, living and working on the island of Bali in Indonesia where he is a partner in 'Tropical Line', a company of landscape design; he is a specialist in water gardens.

Michael lives in Dublin and has his own company called 'Pettigrew Interior Plants'. He does voluntary work in the Glencree Centre for Reconciliation in County Wicklow and is also training to be a therapist in bio-energy healing.